# Tudor W

*Edited by*

*Trevor Herbert*
*Gareth Elwyn Jones*

Cardiff
University of Wales Press
1988

University of Wales Press, 6 Gwennyth Street, Cathays, Cardiff CF2 4YD



**British Library Cataloguing in Publication Data**

Tudor Wales : Welsh history and its sources.
1. Wales—History 2. Great Britain—History—Tudor period, 1485–1603
I. Herbert, Trevor II. Jones, Gareth Elwyn
942.905 DA720

ISBN 0-7083-0971-2



Cover design : Cloud Nine Design

The publishers wish to acknowledge the advice and assistance given by the Design Department of the Welsh Books Council which is supported by the Welsh Arts Council.

Printed in Wales by Graham Harcourt (Printers) Ltd, Swansea

WELSH HISTORY AND ITS SOURCES

# Tudor Wales

# *Welsh History and its Sources*

Welsh History and its Sources is a project conducted at the Open University in Wales form 1985 to 1988 and funded by a Welsh Office Research Development grant. The project gratefully acknowledges the financial support made available by the Secretary of State for Wales.

| | |
|---|---|
| Project Director: | Dr Trevor Herbert |
| Senior Visiting Fellow: | Dr Gareth Elwyn Jones |
| Steering Committee: | Mr O.E. Jones, H.M.I. (Chairman)<br>Professor R.R. Davies, History Department, University College of Wales, Aberystwyth<br>Mr N. Evans, Coleg Harlech<br>Mr D. Maddox, Advisor, Mid Glamorgan LEA<br>Mr A. Evans, Head of History Department, Y Pant Comprehensive School, Pontyclun |
| Secretary to the Project at the Open University in Wales: | Mrs Julia Williams |

# Contents

# *Illustrations*

# *Maps and Diagrams*

# *Contributors*

DR MATTHEW GRIFFITHS is an Investigator for the Royal Commission on Ancient Monuments in Wales and an Open University course tutor for course A203, *Seventeenth-century England: a changing culture 1618–1689*.

DR TREVOR HERBERT is Senior Lecturer in Music at the Open University and Staff Tutor in Arts at the Open University in Wales.

MR BRIAN HOWELLS was formerly Senior Lecturer in the History of Wales at the University College of Wales, Aberystwyth,

DR GARETH ELWYN JONES is Reader in History Education at University College of Swansea and an Open University tutor-counsellor for the arts foundation course.

DR GWYNFOR JONES is Senior Lecturer in the History of Wales at University College, Cardiff.

PROFESSOR GLANMOR WILLIAMS is Professor Emeritus in History at University College of Swansea.

DR PENRY WILLIAMS is a Fellow of New College, Oxford.

# *Preface*

This series gives an insight into Welsh history by examining its sources and the ways in which some leading historians use those sources. It is not formally a history of Wales. This volume, for instance, is not a chronological history of Wales in the Tudor period, neither is it a comprehensive history in the sense that its themes embrace all of the major issues and events that were important in that period. Readers of this book will, we hope, learn a great deal about Wales in the sixteenth century but they will learn as much about the way in which professional historians interpret the raw materials of history.

The choice of topics reflects the editors' view of central themes in the period. Those themes also tell us much about the nature of the evidence available to the historian. Far more than is the case for later periods, we have to rely on a relatively restricted range of sources. It will become apparent, for example, that Tudor gentry themselves contributed substantially to the literary evidence of the time, so that all our contributors draw on George Owen's *Description of Penbrockshire.* Gwynfor Jones and Brian Howells therefore have to take into account that substantial parts of their evidence reflect a gentry view of social strata, though they also use statistics where these can be found. Matthew Griffiths is similarly placed in relation to his sources and has to confront the problem of the extreme difficulty of securing reliable statistical material, demographic or economic. Glanmor Williams faces a different but similarly intractable problem. How does the historian begin to unravel the complexities of popular belief among a largely unlettered population? The poetry of the bards helps, but its use begs many questions. Penry Williams, though having the basic facts provided by such stalwart sources as statutes, confronts as emotive an issue as exists in the history of Wales.

At one level *Tudor Wales* is simply a book about a particular period in the history of Wales and about the ways in which historians interpret that period. However, the series of which this volume is a part has been designed to serve a number of functions for anyone who is formally or informally engaged in a study of Welsh history. Those studying with a tutor, for instance extra-mural, university or sixth-form students, will find that it is a resource which will form a basis for, or enhance, a broader study of Welsh history. Those who are studying in a more remote location, far from formal classes in Welsh history, will find that the contents of the book are so ordered as to guide them through a course of study similar, but not analogous, to the methods which have proved successful in continuing education programmes of the Open University. The main feature of this method is that it attempts to combine a programmatic approach with something more flexible and open-ended.

Central to this book are Sections A-E which contain three different but closely-related and interlinked types of material. Five essays are written on clearly-defined topics. Each essay is immediately followed by a collection of source material which is the basis of the evidence for the essay. Within each essay, reference is made to a particular source document by the inclusion of a reference number in the essay text; this reference number is also placed in the left-hand margin of the essay.

Each section contains a discussion of the topic under the heading **Debating the Evidence**. The primary purpose here is to highlight the special features, weaknesses and strengths of each collection of sources and to question the way in which the author of the essay has used them. It is worth pointing out that we have not attempted here simply to act as *agents provocateurs*, setting up a series of artificial controversies which can be comfortably demolished. The purpose is to raise the sorts of questions which essayists themselves probably addressed before they employed these sources. In doing this we hope to expose the types of issues that the historian has to deal with. The discussion sections pose a number of questions about the sources. They do not provide model answers and neatly tie up all of the loose ends concerning each source. The discipline of history does not allow that approach. If it did, there would be no need for a book of this type. The 'discussions' simply put forward a number of ideas which will cause readers to consider and reconsider the issues which have been raised. The purpose is to breed the kind of healthy scepticism about historical sources which underlies the method of approach of the professional historian.

Other parts of the book support these central sections. The Introduction poses basic problems about the difficulties of coping with historical sources, points which are consolidated in the Discussion sections. The intention of the first essay, *Tudor Wales*, is to highlight immediately some seminal issues confronting the historian of the sixteenth century. We witness an organic mythology at work as Henry VII assumes an Arthurian mantle and we confront some of the implications of historical periodization. At the end of the book is a glossary which briefly explains a number of the more technical terms and concepts arising out of the essays/documents collection. Although a glossary is properly a list of explanations of words and terms, we have, additionally, included brief details of persons who figure prominently in the essay and documents material. Such words and names are *italicized* (thus) and are explained in the glossary.

Readers will, of course, decide how best to profit from the different constituent elements in the book. The first two essays should certainly be read first, as these provide a context for the rest of the book. Some may then decide to read the five essays without reference to the source collections or discussion sections. This will form a broader framework for a re-examination of the essays with their sources and discussion sections.

The open-ended nature of the book serves to highlight the extent to which it has been our intention to do no more than *contribute* to an understanding of Welsh history. Different editors would have chosen different topics. The essays here should be seen within the framework of a much wider range of writings which, over the past few decades, has become available. The greatest success which a book like this can meet with is that it imparts to its readers an insatiable desire to know more about Welsh history and to do so from a standpoint which is constantly and intelligently questioning the ways in which historians provide that knowledge.

# *Acknowledgements*

The development of the Welsh History and its Sources project was made possible by the support of the Secretary of State for Wales and I am happy to have made formal acknowledgement to the Secretary of State and individuals connected with the project elsewhere in this book.

Funding from the Open University made possible the development of the initial ideas that were eventually nurtured by a Welsh Office grant. The assistance of various individuals and departments of the Open University has been frequently and freely given. In particular, my colleagues at the Open University in Wales, where the project was based, have been constantly helpful. Julia Williams, secretary to the Arts Faculty of the Open University in Wales, acted as secretary to the project. As well as word processing the texts for the entire series she was immensely efficient in the administration of the project. Picture copyright research was carried out by Rhodri Morgan. Editing for the University of Wales Press was done by Anne Howells and the Index compiled by Annette Musker.

University College, Swansea, were kind enough to allow the part secondment of Dr Gareth Elwyn Jones to work on the project. Without him the project would not have progressed beyond being an idea as I have relied entirely on his widely-respected expertise for overseeing the academic content of the series.

Diverse contributions have enhanced the effectiveness of the material. Guy Lewis, University College, Swansea, drew the maps and diagrams, often from a jumble of data and instructions. E.D. Evans made an important contribution to Discussion sections of the *Wales 1880–1914* volume of this series. That volume was developmentally tested in 1984 and advice gained from this piloting was particularly helpful. It was undertaken by Neil Evans, colleagues and students at Coleg

Harlech and by David Maddox, Christopher Despres, Raymond Bevan, Hefin Matthias, Kenneth Morgan, John Wilson, colleagues and students from Mid Glamorgan County Council's Education Department.

My major debt of gratitude is to the contributors, each of whom was asked to write to a prescribed topic, format, word length and submission date. Each fulfilled his brief with absolute accuracy, punctuality and co-operation. The format was prescribed by me. Any shortcomings that this book may have can be put down to that prescription and to the consequences that emanated from it.

TREVOR HERBERT

*Cardiff*
*October 1986*

# *Introduction*

The essays contained in this book have been written not only by specialist historians, but also by specialists in the particular topic on which they have written. They are authorities on their subject and they make pertinent, informed and professional observations. Each essay is an important contribution to the historiography of Wales.

As specialists they know the sources for their topics intimately. They have included extracts from a cross-section of these sources to indicate on what evidence they base the generalizations and conclusions in their essays. We hope that the essays will interest you and that the documents will bring you into contact with the kinds of primary sources which you may not have encountered before. Historians face a variety of problems when they consult source material and face even more difficulties when they have to synthesize the material collected into a coherent narrative and analysis of the events they are describing. In doing so even the best historians make mistakes. Sometimes these are trivial (or not so trivial!) errors of fact. You may even spot factual discrepancies between information given in the various essays and the documents in this book.

At the end of each essay/sources section there is a short discussion section. By the time you reach it you will have read the essay and the sources on which the essay is based.

The discussion.section is concerned with problems of interpretation. It is an attempt to conduct a debate with the author about the way in which the essay relates to the sources. This is partly achieved by asking pertinent questions about the nature of the sources themselves. The intention is that you are stimulated to think about the validity of the exercise of writing history and the methodology of the study of history which is essentially what distinguishes it from other disciplines. The dialogue is a complex one and the questions posed do not, generally, have any 'right' answers. But they do have some answers which make more sense than others. We hope that the historians who have written the essays have provided answers which are reasonable. But historians are not infallible, however eminent they may be. Their conclusions are open to debate and discussion, as, for that matter, is their whole procedure of working. As you work through the discussion and questions you will notice that there is specific cross-referencing to the relevant section of the essay (or essays) and to documents. We hope this will be helpful since the success of the exercise depends vitally on taking into account the relationship between the primary source material and what the historian makes of it.

At the heart of the historian's task is the search for and subsequent use of evidence, much of it of the sort you will encounter here. The crucial distinction in the nature of this evidence is that between primary and secondary sources. There is no completely watertight definition of primary sources but a reasonable working definition would be that primary sources consist of material which came into existence during the period which the historian is researching, while secondary sources came into existence after that period. Whether or not a source can be regarded as primary or secondary relies as much on the topic of research as it does on the date of that source.

For example, if we consider the first of Gwynfor Jones's sources (A.1) it is an extract from William Williams's *History of the Bulkeley Family*. It was published in 1674 which, strictly, means that it is a *secondary* source for the Tudor period. Certainly it was written centuries ago but it is well outside the Tudor period which ended in 1603. This distancing in time is significant because it means that the author would be unlikely to have been personally acquainted with Sir Richard Bulkeley, though he might well have had access to many who had known him. It remains that, for Tudor Wales, this is a secondary source. However, if we were researching into the history of the writing of biographies or family histories from, say, 1500-1900 then Williams's *History* becomes a primary source, and the questions we would ask of it would be very different in emphasis, as would be the answers we would glean.

Historical interpretation based on the sources is extremely complex. It was once believed by highly reputable historians that if they mastered all the sources they could write 'true' history. There is at least one eminent historian who argues this now. You might like to consider on which side of the debate you stand at the moment.

Most historians would argue that this is impossible, that because we are removed from the time and place of the event that we are considering we are influenced by prejudices of nationality, religion or politics. However, there is some compensation for this because we know, usually, what the results were of actions which occurred during the period we are considering and this benefit of hindsight is enormously useful in trying to analyse the interplay of various factors in a situation and their influence on subsequent events. As you read the essays and documents in this collection, consider the degree of objectivity and subjectivity displayed by the authors. To do this you will need to consider what you would like to know about the authors before coming to a decision and how far the authors are entitled to their own interpretations.

There is a similar pattern of work for each essay and its related documents. There are specific questions involving comprehension, evaluation, interpretation and synthesis, with synthesis, arguably, the highest level of the skills. However, there can be no rigid demarcation of historical skills such as interpretation and synthesis and some questions will overlap the various categories. There is no standard form of 'answer' either as the discussions demonstrate. What the questions do provide is a structured pattern of work which will enhance understanding of the essays and documents.

Above all, there is dialogue and discussion about the way in which each historian has grappled with the complexities of writing about and interpreting the past. That such interpretation is as skilled, informed and mature as is conceivably possible is essential to our well-being as a society. In that these books are about the history of Wales they contribute fundamentally to the well-being of Welsh society. That well-being depends on debate, analytical, informed, structured debate. It is the purpose of this book to stimulate your involvement in that debate in a more structured way than has been attempted before in the study of the history of Wales.

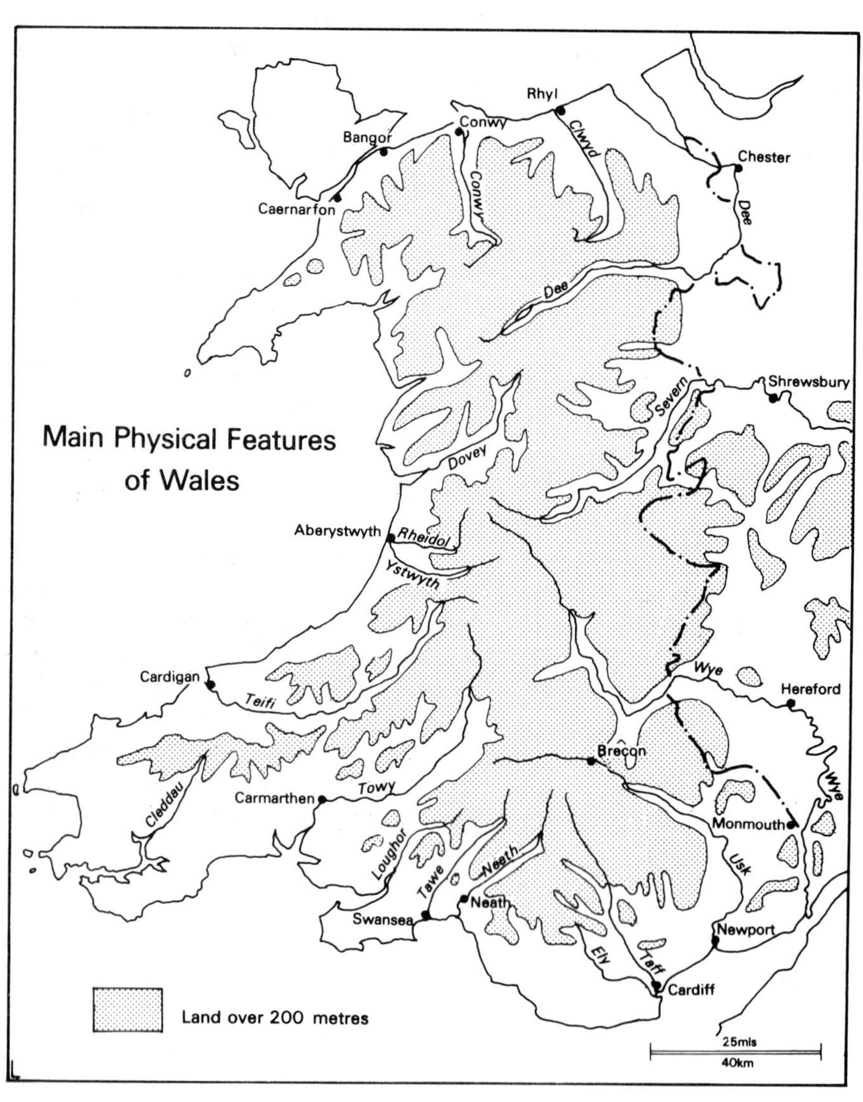

Main Physical Features of Wales
Rhyl
Conwy
Bangor
Caernarfon
Chester
Clwyd
Conwy
Dee
Dee
Shrewsbury
Severn
Dovey
Aberystwyth
Rheidol
Ystwyth
Cardigan
Teifi
Wye
Hereford
Brecon
Wye
Carmarthen
Towy
Cleddau
Monmouth
Loughor
Neath
Tawe
Usk
Neath
Swansea
Newport
Ely
Taff
Cardiff
Land over 200 metres
25mls
40km

# *Timechart*

| Wales | | Other Significant Events |
|---|---|---|
| | **1066** | Norman Conquest of England. |
| Death of Llywelyn ap Gruffudd, the last native Prince of Wales | **1282** | |
| Principality of Wales comes into existence by the terms of the Statute of Wales. | **1284** | |
| Start of Owain Glyndŵr's rising. | **1400** | |
| Birth of Henry Tudor. | **1457** | |
| Creation of Council in Marches of Wales. | **1471** | |
| Henry Tudor's unsuccessful invasion of Wales and England. | **1483** | |
| Battle of Bosworth. | **1485** | Henry Tudor becomes King (Henry VII). |

| Wales | Year | England |
|---|---|---|
| Bishop William Barlow born. | **1499** | |
| | **1501** | Marriage of Prince Arthur and Catherine of Aragon. Death of Prince Arthur, Henry VII's heir. |
| Bishop Richard Davies born. | *c.***1501** | |
| Sir John Price born. | *c.***1502** | |
| | **1506** | Birth of John Leland, the King's Antiquary in the reign of Henry VIII. |
| | **1509** | Henry VIII becomes King. Marries Catherine of Aragon. |
| | **1515** | Thomas Wolsey becomes Chancellor. |
| William Salesbury born. Dr David Lewis born. | *c.***1520** | |
| Sir Edward Stradling born. | **1525** | |
| | *c.***1532** | Earl of Leicester born. |
| | **1532** | Thomas Cromwell becomes chief minister to Henry VIII. |
| | **1533** | England breaks with the Pope. |
| Rowland Lee sent to Wales as President of the Council in the Marches. | **1534** | Henry VIII becomes Supreme Head of the Church of England. |

| Wales | Year | England |
|---|---|---|
| | **1535** | Act of Succession. |
| First Act of Union. Dissolution of almost all Welsh monasteries. | **1536** | Dissolution of the wealthier English monasteries. |
| Shrines and centres of pilgrimage abolished. | **1538** | |
| | **1539** | Dissolution of the lesser English monasteries. |
| Burning of Thomas Capper for heresy. | **1542/3** | |
| Sir William Maurice of Clenennau born. | **1542** | |
| Second Act of Union. | **1543** | |
| Bishop William Morgan born. | *c.*1545 | |
| First printed book in Welsh — *Yn y lhyvyr Hwnn.* | **1546** | |
| William Salesbury's book of proverbs: *Oll Synnwyr Pen.* | **1547** | Death of Henry VIII. Edward VI becomes King at the age of nine. |
| | **1549** | First Book of Common Prayer. |
| Sir William Herbert made Earl of Pembroke. | **1551** | |
| George Owen of Henllys born. | *c.*1552 | |

| Wales | Year | England |
| --- | --- | --- |
| | **1552** | Second Book of Common Prayer. |
| Birth of Sir John Wynn of Gwydir. | **1553** | Death of Edward VI. Lady Jane Grey Queen for nine days. Mary I becomes Queen. |
| Bishop Ferrar burned as heretic in Carmarthen. Death of Sir John Price. | **1555** | |
| | **1558** | Loss of Calais. Elizabeth I becomes Queen. Sir William Cecil becomes chief minister. |
| Death of Sir Rice Mansel of Margam. Sir Henry Sidney becomes President of the Council in the Marches. | **1559** | |
| Act for the translation of the Bible into Welsh. John Penry born. | **1563** | Statute of Artificers passed. |
| | **1566** | Earl of Essex born. |
| Publication of *New Testament* in Welsh. | **1567** | |
| Death of Bishop Barlow. | **1568** | |
| Sir Richard Bulkeley of Beaumaris becomes head of his family. | **1572** | |

| Wales | Date | Elsewhere |
|---|---|---|
| | **1577–80** | Drake sails around the world. |
| Death of Bishop Richard Davies. | **1581** | |
| Richard Gwyn executed for his Roman Catholic faith. Death of Dr David Lewis. | **1584** | |
| Death of William Salesbury. | *c.***1584** | |
| Henry Herbert, Earl of Pembroke, becomes President of the Council in the Marches. | **1586** | |
| Death of Rice Merrick of Cottrell. | **1586/7** | |
| | **1587** | Mary, Queen of Scots, executed. |
| Translation of *Bible* into Welsh. | **1588** | The Spanish Armada. Death of Earl of Leicester. |
| Execution of John Penry. | **1593** | |
| Death of Sir Edward Mansel of Margam. | **1595** | |
| | **1601** | Earl of Essex executed. |
| | **1603** | Death of Queen Elizabeth. End of Tudor dynasty. Accession of Stuart dynasty with coronation of James I. |

Humphrey Lhuyd's map of Wales 1573. (*Source: National Library of Wales.*)

# *Tudor Wales*

GARETH ELWYN JONES

This topic has always held the imagination of the Welsh. For example, it has always dominated advanced studies in history in the schools of Wales. It is not difficult to think of reasons. Perhaps the most potent is that, for just over a century, England as well as Wales was ruled over by a dynasty sprung from a Welshman, Henry VII. No matter that the pure Welsh blood of his grandfather, Owen Tudor, mingled in his veins with French and English blood. To important Welshmen of his time Henry VII was Welsh — it suited them well that he should be so. The Venetian ambassador caught contemporary stress on Henry's nationality: 'The Welsh may be said to have recovered their former independence, the most wise and fortunate Henry VII is a Welshman.'

The significance of Henry's descent lay not in sentimental national pride — a regal variety of rugby-international enthusiasm. Henry was heir to a vital historical tradition which had succoured influential Welshmen through long years of defeat. To the Welsh poets, honoured recounters of tradition, Henry was the long-promised heir to Brutus the Trojan who, according to Geoffrey of Monmouth's *Historia Regum Britanniae*, had originally ruled over the island of Britain. He was the new *Arthur*, that *Arthur* who was the legendary leader of the Britons against the Saxons. The potency of this mythology was enormous in late medieval Wales — and shows how significant mythology can be as a historical force. With Geoffrey of Monmouth, it was easy to picture a once-united Britain ruled over by the ancestors of the Welsh. The story had it that they had been defeated, certainly, but only by treachery. After intricate and deep-laid plots running the gamut of conquest and love-interest, Saxon leader Hengist and his men had treacherously murdered British leader Vortigern's nobles at a banquet, after which Vortigern had no option but to yield up much of eastern Britain to the Saxons. The significance of this legend in Welsh history is well attested — it was readily understood as late as the nineteenth century. Being vanquished by treachery endowed the Welsh with a moral right to the throne of Britain (England and Wales). A new leader would come. Unfortunately in the real world leaders tended to disappoint. The achievements of Llywelyn the Great and Llywelyn the Last in the thirteenth century culminated in massive, decisive defeat in 1282–3 by Edward I. Welsh independence was at an end. Another folk hero did once emerge. In the years after 1400 *Owain Glyndŵr* transformed a feudal quarrel into a crusade for Welsh independence. Here, indeed, was the new leader foretold. Sadly, he too was vanquished, though his mysterious disappearance in the wake of defeat (no-one knows where or when he died) allowed the idea to prevail that he would return.

The intermittent civil wars of the fifteenth century, the *Wars of the Roses*, had a Welsh dimension in the prophetic poetry of the Welsh *bards*. They fastened on to a succession of claimants to the throne as being fit repositories for the pent-up emotional frustrations of centuries of defeat and humiliation. But the Welsh (British) claims of Henry Tudor were tailor-made. By an unlikely series of events the grandson of a minor Anglesey gentleman who had been taken on at court and married the French-born widow of English King Henry V, found himself king after the *Battle of Bosworth*. The prophecy was fulfilled. The *bardic* sentiment which fastened on to Henry Tudor as heir to tradition and legend has never been entirely dissipated. For many students the Tudor dynasty remains the Welsh dynasty. 'Tudor Wales' remains a popular and nicely-packaged period, and merely by giving it this traditional label some seminal questions relating to the study of history have been brought up. The relationship between myth and history is a fascinating one. The prophetic tradition which accumulated around Henry Tudor is one of those 'organic' myths which actually had an impact in moulding opinion and contributing to Henry's success in his bid for the throne. Not that its effects should be overestimated. The historical moment was apt. Henry Tudor's hard-headed, even ambivalent, supporters, were not seduced by historical tradition but attracted by solid self-interest. Yet there is no gainsaying that in this significant episode the main guardians of the Welsh cultural heritage, the *bards*, provide evidence that they felt a prophecy to have been fulfilled and a new era to have dawned for the Welsh.

Llyna feirdd yn llawenach
Llwyddo'r byd a lladd
R. Bach . . .
Harri fu, harry a fo,
Harri sydd, hir oes iddo.

'Here are bards much happier, the world is all the better for killing little R. . . . Harry was, will be and now is; long life to him.'
(Quoted in Glanmor Williams, *Henry Tudor and Wales*, Cardiff, 1985, p.61.)

The role of mythology and tradition is particularly fascinating in Welsh history. This has been because they have had to compensate so often for defeat and disillusionment. Investigating their impact is particularly difficult because all the evidence is literary. Geoffrey of Monmouth's *Historia Regum Britanniae* was invention masquerading as history. Its impact, which as we have seen was considerable, has to be assessed in what may seem an unlikely historical source, poetry. Considerable specialist knowledge is involved, since this poetry is replete with symbolism. More than this, the historian using such sources has to be immersed in the period before being able to judge accurately their nuances of historical meaning. Yet such sources are absolutely vital for the medieval and Tudor periods in gauging reaction to political and religious developments in particular.

### From poetry to periodization

It is obvious that the Tudor period runs from the accession of the first Tudor in 1485 to the death of the last, Elizabeth I in 1603. But that title 'Tudor Wales', seemingly so innocuous, so neutral, reveals a view of history, an imposed interpretation, before we even get on to any content. First it reveals a dynastic view of history, taking as its focal points the reigns of monarchs and, by implication, regarding their initiatives and policies as the motor of change. Such assumptions would have been entirely appropriate to the historiography of the nineteenth century which stressed political history above all else. Perhaps it is now making something of a comeback. But in general terms, recent historical investigation has centred on a much more widely-based analysis of economic and social change, and attempts to reconstruct the role of the mass of the people in the historical process. This is not easy. The evidence is never complete, of course, but it abounds for kings and queens, their councils and their policies, their dress and their hunting habits, their tennis and their courtly rituals. Their portraits perform a political purpose when, as with Elizabeth I, they are full of the symbolism of 'gloriana', so there tend to be a lot of them. There are no portraits of labourers or small tenant farmers and precious few documents to recall details of their lives. However since, for a variety of reasons, we rightly regard them as being as significant as their monarchs, historians are intent on rescuing them from the oblivion to which they were for so long consigned. For such groups as these, 1485 or 1603 made precious little difference. The tempo of their lives was affected by far different social and economic trends which demand a wholely different chronology in Wales as in England.

Even if we revert to a 'monarchist' view of history there are complications because historians have placed Henry VII at the centre of a 'medieval/modern' controversy, so focusing attention more starkly on these dividing lines. Such periodization is an invention. While traditionally historians have labelled the years up to 1485 'medieval' and the years between 1485 and the industrial revolution 'early modern', there is a fundamental unreality here. Such labels could have no meaning for contemporary observers. Still, it is the historian's task to impose some pattern on inordinately complex and inter-relating past events. The *nature* of that pattern is a matter of as much debate as the tale which is eventually told. We have had Whig, Marxist, main-line, conservative, and revisionist schools of historians at work on the Tudor period.

By our selection of topics for the essays which follow we, as editors, have revealed that we regard certain matters as being of central importance in the history of Tudor Wales. The focus for us is Wales, so we are less exercised as to whether Henry VII was the last of the 'medievals' or the first of the 'moderns'. Let us turn to the reign of Henry VIII. Probably it was *Thomas Cromwell*, Henry VIII's chief minister, who was responsible for inaugurating the policy which brought about the Union of England and Wales by means of two major acts in 1536 and 1543. The union of two countries, particularly when it was intended to integrate the political, legal and administrative systems, and to make English the official language of a largely monoglot Welsh-speaking nation, is obviously an event of momentous significance. It was no partnership between equals. Wales was very much a minor partner, the conquered nation still suffering, at least by letter of the law, from penal legislation consequent on the *Glyndŵr Revolt* which made the

Welsh second-class citizens in their own country. The union has been permanent. Not surprisingly it has occasioned all manner of historical controversies since. In so doing it has considerably illuminated the nature of the exercise in which the historian is engaged. In the first place it bears on the matter with which we were lately concerned, that of periodization. A view of Welsh history which concentrates on Henry VII as heir to the poetic tradition of the middle ages, the son of prophecy, a Welsh avenger of Welsh defeats, the new king of the Britons, first of a Welsh dynasty which brought order out of chaos and restored self-respect to the Welsh, would still stress the validity of the label 'Tudor Wales'. According to this view the *Acts of Union* might be seen as part of a *process* of integration of the two countries on equal terms, inaugurated by Henry's victory at *Bosworth*. According to this view Henry Tudor was the man who restored Welsh self-respect by welcoming the Welsh at court, adopting the red dragon of *Cadwaladr*, last king of the Britons, as his standard and naming his eldest son *Arthur*.

It is not now fashionable to take this view and see 1485 as a significant dividing line. A history of modern Wales would probably be more likely now to start with the first *Act of Union*, 1536 — the convenient conjunction here is that the *Acts of Union* can be seen as part of the Tudor 'revolution in government', as one of the most eminent of Tudor historians has dubbed it — that period of administrative reform masterminded by *Thomas Cromwell* which saw at least the administrative transition in England and Wales from a medieval to a more modern state. According to this view the union of Wales with England can be seen as part of a fundamental tidying up in which a country with a mixture of government, laws and authority became part of an efficient, powerful, unified and administratively coherent wider realm.

More important,to the Welsh historian *per se*, this event can assume an overriding importance since it brought about the integration of two countries in which Wales, as the weaker partner, was bound to succumb to an economically powerful and dominant state. At the extreme end of this spectrum comes the view that the *Acts of Union* were a deliberate attempt to cast Wales into oblivion — its laws, customs, society and above all, language, an act of unparalleled vandalism in attempting to destroy an ancient nation. The point is, then, that by the simple act of pinning the label 'Tudor Wales' on to this book we have opened up a controversy which encompasses the historiography of England and

Wales, and arouses burning passions among Welsh historians. That simple labelling leads to many an insight into the historical discipline. It reveals a concern with evidence, with sources, certainly, but also with the role of myth in history, with patriotism and, generally, with the complexity of historical periodization, generalizations and judgements.

That wider controversy is fashioned from many minor ones. Welsh society after the *Acts of Union* was dominated by landowners — the gentry. Their economic resources were translated into dominance of local government and the local community, even if, relatively, they were considerably less prosperous than their English counterparts. They were the people who could afford an education, and, increasingly, valued it. They were the literate members of society and the ones with some leisure time. Inevitably they are the group who have left written evidence of reactions to the Tudor dynasty and the impact of the *Acts of Union.* Until relatively recently it was their view of Tudor Wales which held sway — and to some extent still does. They portray a Wales cast down, defeated and chaotic before the advent of the Tudors. Then came what George Owen (*A Dialogue of the Government of Wales*, 1594) called the 'joyful metamorphosis' wrought by Henry Tudor, 'a Moses that delivered us from bondage', 'a prince of our own nation and born in our country', who inaugurated a period of order and good government for Wales, consolidated by the *Acts of Union.* Distortion is inevitable in the sixteenth century by the very nature of the social structure. The unlettered labourer and tenant left no direct testimony of this sort — but the distortion of gentry judgements is compounded when we take into account that it was precisely this class which benefited most from Tudor policy — particularly that of Union. It was the gentry whose alliance with the monarchy guaranteed the stability of the Tudor state at local level. It was the gentry who ensured that local administration worked and justice was administered. These responsibilities cemented the position of the gentry in their community. Not surprisingly they regarded such developments favourably. In modifying the picture left by Tudor gentry writers and attempting to look critically at some of their literary evidence the historian is merely doing his job of examining the historical record sceptically, attempting to weigh up the biases of contemporary observers. But historical evaluation is not just a matter of clinical assessment. The historian then brings his or her own bias to bear, and this is conditioned not by Tudor society but by the society of which the historian is a part. That society has changed dramatically in the recent past with the changing nature of Welsh nationalism in the twentieth century. Especially after the Second World War, Welsh political nationalism developed, to culminate in some heady triumphs in the 1960s and 1970s. Concern over the fate of the Welsh language has grown steadily this century. Practical results have been as varied as widespread Welsh-medium education, full official status for the Welsh language and direct action to secure road signs in Welsh and the establishment of a predominantly Welsh-medium television channel. Inevitably, Welsh nationalists are historians, though not necessarily professional ones. They look to the past for authority and succour. Inevitably, they look to that Tudor century of the *Acts of Union* which, legally, did away with Wales as a separate entity ('incorporated, united and annexed to and with this . . . Realm of England') and decreed that 'henceforth no Person or Persons that use the Welsh Speech or Language shall have or enjoy any Manner, Office or Fees within this Realm of England'. For some committed nationalist writers the verdict is clear. Gwynfor Evans, charismatic president of Plaid Cymru, judged that as a result of Tudor policies 'it was England that lived purposefully; in Wales all feeling of purpose was finished, apart from serving its big neighbour. A host of Welshmen received personal advancement but their country deteriorated and gradually decayed.' The personal advancement, of course, was that of the gentry, and nationalist professional historians would, perhaps less stridently, endorse this judgement. Other Welsh historians would argue that judgements of this kind are anachronistic in that they impose twentieth-century predilections on wholly different sixteenth-century conceptions of state, society and nationalism.

The nationalist controversy is by no means the only one to impinge on the study of Tudor Wales, though it is the most emotive one now. Some generations ago it might have been argued that the religious state of Wales in Tudor times gave rise to most controversy. Like nationalism, religious commitment is an amorphous and elastic concept. How might it be measured? By numbers of martyrs, or *recusants*, or attendance at church, or the outpourings of the new printing press or the anti-clericalism of some Welsh poets, or numbers of monks in monasteries? If we think of the range of evidence here the task of the historian is complex indeed. He has the *Valor Ecclesiasticus* to provide him with details of numbers of monks in monasteries, but has that given him evidence of the depth of their religious commitment? He has to take into account the evidence of *Thomas Cromwell*'s visitors who reported on conditions in the monasteries in the knowledge that their master wanted evidence which would legitimize the closure of the monasteries. Little evidence remains by which we can assess the nature of popular belief and attitudes, except in one of the most difficult sources of all, the poetry of the *bards*. If we set these difficulties in the context of the century which saw the break with Rome and the *dissolution of the monasteries* under Henry VIII, and the establishment of the Church of England under Elizabeth I, it is not surprising that historians committed to the Roman Catholic or Protestant cause should have produced widely different accounts both of Tudor policy and the state of religious belief and practice. Only relatively recently has a greater degree of a consensus emerged with the modification of entrenched denominational hostilities.

Some of the complexities of the historian's task have emerged in this discussion of three linked emotive topics — mythology, nationalism and religion. In discussing them we have highlighted some of the implications of historians imposing interpretations on the past — by labelling periods, selecting topics or constructing generalizations. The broad framework of the material on Tudor Wales which follows has been imposed by the editors who perhaps betray some of their own attitudes in so doing. However, within that context, the essayists have come to grips with their own topic in their own way. It will emerge that they have had to cope with very different kinds of sources, all of them in some way deficient, all of them posing their own problems of interpretation. In reading these essays, in conjunction with the sources which the authors have worked on, you will encounter historians providing a great deal of information about Tudor Wales. Through this they provide an insight into the historian's craft. To sum up, we can do no better than use the words, slightly adapted, of one of the contributors, Glanmor Williams, in his book on *Henry Tudor* :

> No final answers to great historical questions can be found or expected. Each new generation will continue to ask those questions of the past which it believes to be the most relevant and important, and will answer them in the light of its own knowledge and principles. Part of the answer will come from its experience of the present as well as its knowledge of the past. Since individuals and generations differ from one another in their attitudes, so their answers, too, will be bound to differ. But the task

confronting the historian will remain the same: to search for the information as widely, accurately and objectively as he can; to describe as truthfully as possible what happened; and to discuss honestly and sympathetically what people living at the time and since have thought and felt about it. There is no 'last word' to be spoken on this or any other historical topic.

# *The Gentry*

GWYNFOR JONES

The social and economic development of Wales over a century and a half before the Tudor period saw the long and protracted 'rise of the gentry' and the emergence in the social structure of the Principality and the *March* of a new order out of the dislocation caused by economic changes. It was this new order that was to assume prominence in all aspects of community life and to dominate Wales in the sixteenth century. Most of the documentary material available for that period reveals the ways and means by which these new families had acquired, augmented, maintained and protected their properties against the claims of tenants and other competitors. The evidence also testifies to their aims and ambitions as well as describing significant aspects of their lifestyle, cultural interests and social contacts.

The Tudor gentry — or *uchelwyr* — constituted those who, by rank and status had, in varying degrees, attained positions of respect and authority. They could generally be divided into two main categories. The first group, which formed the larger of the two, were descendants of free clansmen whose ancestors, in the early Middle Ages, had abandoned their nomadic habits and had settled permanently upon *clanlands* in the uplands of Wales. Their successors were gentry of native Welsh stock who had claimed their rights to properties on the basis of hereditary succession and a good reputable ancestry. During the years extending approximately between the Black Death in the mid-fourteenth century and the advent of the Tudors — a period of vast economic change and disruption — free clansmen emerged who were in the process of breaking away from *the kindred system* and who had acquired a stake in property other than that which had been granted to them by *partible inheritance*. It was they who laid the basis of forward-looking families on the up-grade who grasped at every opportunity to avoid their obligations to Welsh land law and to acquire the rights and privileges which Englishmen enjoyed free of the restrictions imposed by kindred custom. Wherever possible they would occupy the lands and rights of less fortunate kinsmen who, owing to economic stress, found it impossible to maintain their clan privileges in land and who were forced to yield their properties. It was these lands which, in time, formed a substantial part of new private estates owned by capitalistic country gentry.

The second group of property-owners were the descendants of Norman English immigrant families which had moved, from the late eleventh and twelfth centuries onwards, into Welsh boroughs and had prospered by trade and commercial dealings as well as by
A.1 prudent marriages into local Welsh families (A.1). It was an age of transition in the Principality and *March* alike from the old medieval subsistence economy to the growth of landed estates based on capitalism. Ancient *feudal dues* in *the March* gave way to the gradual formation of consolidated farms. In spite of the *Glyndŵr Revolt* and its bitter legacies of racial animosities and distrust, the accumulation of lands in the possession of aggressive county and urban gentry became one of the prime features of Welsh social and economic development in the fifteenth century. Some dominant families had established themselves in various parts of Wales and *the March* long before Henry Tudor came to the English throne in 1485.

The sixteenth-century Welsh gentry were composed of a very broad stratum of modest freeholders whose chief claim to gentility was reputable ancestry. They extended from knights and esquires at the top end of the scale down to gentlemen and *yeomen* farmers. As a status symbol lineage and its ramifications were valued above all else. They were one of the principal means of proving title to property and inheritance since the Tudor Settlement (1536–43) which had formally adopted the practice of *primogeniture* as the method of succession to land. The dynastic approach to the consolidation of estates, aided largely by the use of heraldry and genealogy, was regarded as having been one of the main buttresses against the pretensions of rivals and their claims to a stake in property. The more progressive among the rising

gentry deplored the practices of their forbears in the late Middle Ages who preserved customary Welsh methods of landholding, namely *cyfran* (*partible inheritance*) which increasingly restricted the individual's stake in land and sadly affected his status and material
A.2 prospects (A.2). So depressingly inadequate were the financial means of the majority of Welsh freeholders on the eve of the Tudor Settlement that Rowland Lee, Lord President of the *Council in the Marches*, was prompted to advise the government that they
A.3 were unworthy to hold office (A.3). The physical features of the Welsh countryside was more appropriately geared to maintaining a stock-rearing economy; rent incomes were largely dependent on social and economic conditions which often adversely affected impoverished tenants, and the efforts of tenacious and ambitious gentry, determined to follow the main chance and to keep abreast of their prosperous counterparts elsewhere, were often hindered by a backward economy.

In spite of these less heartening features the most virile among the Welsh gentry, such as the Stradlings of St Donat's, the Morgans of Llantarnam, the Vaughans of Golden Grove, the Mostyns of Flintshire, the Salusburys of Llyweni, the Bulkeleys of Anglesey and the Wynns of Gwydir prospered through the acquisition of land, office and aristocratic patronage as well as by exercising rights which they considered to be theirs by virtue of their traditional status. Their methods of operating were not always considered to be honourable and their accumulation of property was often suspect. Shrewd landowners and their agents, employing all their legal chicanery, sought to undermine tenant rights by seeking out defects in land titles, letting land on short
A.4 leases and raising rents on expiration (A.4), converting *copyhold* to *leasehold* and, on a smaller scale, enclosing common waste land. The Tudor Settlement had facilitated the use of *mortgage* and the most ambitious enhanced their opportunities by purchasing small freehold properties or by encroaching upon and leasing *Crown bond townships*, often in turbulent regions, as did Maredudd ab
A.5 Ieuan, the founder of the Gwydir estate, in Nanconwy (A.5). Others were to prosper by acquiring monastic properties following the dissolution of the religious houses in 1536 or soon after. Added to all this, propitious marriage-settlements and, in several instances, advantageous legal and commercial dealings — all of

Katheryn of Berain — the Llewesog Portrait. (*Source: National Museum of Wales.*)

which often raised the social status of families in the upper income bracket — were also considered to be prime methods of making a family's impact felt in its native environment as well as in the more auspicious surroundings of the royal court and elsewhere.

Such families were aware of the obstacles which could often retard their progress, not the least being the persistence of old clan customs well into the sixteenth century. Ambitious proprietors
A.6 claimed hereditary rights in pastures and wastes (A.6), and it was only by agreement with kinsmen and others who held arable holdings of *clanland* that any consolidation became possible, and that was usually a slow and long process which often created much bad-feeling and the oppression of tenants. Court records testify — often to the point of exaggeration — that forceful defendants were men of great wealth and friendship in their localities and in a position to overawe and dominate their dependants. The gentry who were also Crown farmers took legal action against occupiers who claimed their inheritances, many of which (it was alleged) had been based on fictitious deeds. They also contested the rights of free tenants on manorial lands, particularly the wastes and commons, and were accused of violating rights to common pasture and of enclosing waste, forest and common land which they converted into meadow and arable land.

Regardless of men's greed for land it is a fact that estates were being established, several of them on an ambitious scale. As a result of such acquisitions the gentry built up good reputations for themselves as men of affairs and protectors of their communities. The Tudor Settlement had offered them a new official status whereby they became more eager to prove title to land and enhance their local prestige and authority. Furthermore, strengthening their hold on property had the effect of gradually narrowing the social bracket of the most eligible gentry (with land valued at £1,000 and above) and singling them out as dominant local squires. Family correspondence, for example, reveals the affairs of such people at their broadest and emphasizes the
A.7 sophisticated surroundings in which they lived (A.7). They were at once participants in and contributors to a world where the horizons were set far beyond their neighbourhood and even shire boundary. These sources serve also to show the extent to which

circumstances changed their attitudes and values in their native environment.

Marriage and inheritance were certainly matters of primary importance in any self-respecting family on the up-grade. The marriage of the heir to a rich heiress either in Wales or beyond its borders was considered to be a remarkable achievement because profitable marriage alliances usually buttressed family prestige and added significantly to its material prosperity. Not only did they ensure the future of the estate but also enhanced its fortunes and often raised or consolidated its rank in the local
A.8 community (A.8). The keenest heads of families would avidly search the social market in London and elsewhere for this purpose of maintaining a reputable status. Since *primogeniture* gave priority to the eldest son, the fortunes of younger sons and sisters were primarily governed by their father's financial circumstances. Daughters were usually married off to the heirs of modest local estates and younger sons, whose position often caused embarrassment, were obliged, wherever possible, to seek professional employment in the church, the law, the army or
A.9 trade and commerce (A.9). Several managed to marry local heiresses of lower gentry rank and set up *cadet houses*. Doubtless, marriage, like the institution of the family and household, was considered to be one of the most cohesive social mainstays of gentry life in sixteenth-century England and Wales.

Good breeding and the cultivation of virtues also became the order of the day among affluent families. The impact of the Renaissance in England had yielded to the skilled layman his rightful position in secular society; the quest for education and literacy had become a formative feature of gentry lifestyle, and a high premium was placed on formal instruction and the gracious
A.10 living to which it contributed (A.10). The new Tudor administration, which symbolized the concept of the national sovereign state, demanded the services of able, loyal and educated servants and officials whose aim it was to broaden their intellectual horizons and adopt the same cultural standards and outlook as their English colleagues. This was achieved principally by the founding of privately-endowed grammar schools, and the presence of young gentry at public schools, the Inns of Court and the universities of Oxford and Cambridge. Emphasis was placed

Tombs of the gentry family of the Mansels of Margam, in Margam Abbey Church. (*Source: Glamorgan Archive Service.*)

on a classical curriculum and on cultivating the skills considered
A.11 essential to the English public servant (A.11). Trained administrators would use these skills in furthering the aims of the state and, in their private capacities as heads of households, would be expected to instruct their immediate families in the need to nourish the best qualities and virtues in life.

Equal emphasis was placed on the law and legal training as a means of maintaining an interest in property matters, administering justice in local courts and prosecuting suits concerning property, usually in the central London courts. Litigation had become a frequent and often expensive habit among the most self-seeking gentry in their quest to hold on to all that they owned and to covet what lay within their grasp. The law as a profession was considered to be the most prestigious and lucrative for aspiring younger sons. Indeed Sir Thomas Smith considered that 'whosoever studieth the laws of the realm shall be called master'.[1]

The 'master' usually held a firm grip on his locality. Whatever his evil doings may have been in public life he was still very much a respected figure in his community. Men of power could easily manipulate circumstances and conditions to suit and further their own designs but were often forced to account and pay the penalty for their irregularities. Several, however, were far too strong and were able by sheer force of character to defeat the
A.12 course of law (A.12). For example, John Wyn ap Huw of Bodfel in Llŷn was brought before the *Court of Star Chamber* to answer for his crooked dealings with pirates on Bardsey Island and was described as 'a man of good countenance, great power, ability and friendship in the county'. So powerful was he, in fact, that 'no one will object ought against him or his men, and no jury will indict him'. A hardy man indeed, and many others like him were summoned before the courts to account for their alleged misdeeds usually in connection with property and corruption in public matters. Not that they, in most instances, lost face or were deprived of their status; surprisingly, their family reputation and standing usually remained untarnished. The Clenennau family in Eifionydd, for example, prospered in the days of William Maurice in spite of his father's part in the callous murder of a rival contender for land in that *commote* in 1550. He was indicted

before the *Court of Great Sessions* on a charge of manslaughter but was later released on a mere technicality.

The practice of '*retaining*' and collecting *cymorth*, together with manipulation of legal proceedings, were not considered incompatible with a more staid and progressive lifestyle enjoyed by
A.13 these governing families in their local residences (A.13). The dire forces of inflation from the mid-sixteenth century onwards were to have serious consequences for gentle and ungentle alike. Several were in the firm grip of London moneylenders; their financial commitments in household and other domestic matters alone were heavy and their outlay in legal affairs was likewise quite extensive and often burdensome. Nevertheless, the century saw the building and refurbishing of houses, their architectural features overtly displaying the social climbing of some families which had already shown spirit and tenacity. It was within these houses that broader influences were nourished and they, in due course, were to attract the gentry to more auspicious
A.14 surroundings (A.14).

As the patrons of the well-established *bardic order* and the cultured men of affairs interested in genealogy, heraldry, history and antiquities, they were the chief sustainers of native traditions. Sir John Wynn of Gwydir and *George Owen* of Henllys in Pembrokeshire for example, respectively compiled a family chronicle and a county history and Sir Edward Stradling of St Donat's, arguably the most accomplished of Renaissance figures in the Wales of his day, became a distinguished man of letters while at the same time attending to the routine management of
A.15 his estate (A.15). Such intellectual interests are often reflected in their own private correspondence and notably in formal tributes composed in their honour so profusely by *bards* who visited country seats on a regular basis. There they would obtain hospitality and be remunerated for their grandiloquent odes of praise. Together with the indispensable aid of the gentlewoman of the household whose breeding was every bit as good as that of her husband, charity and entertainment were offered within the *plasty* (mansion house). This mansion, in all its varied aspects, became a focal point of gentility since it symbolized power and authority, beneficence and gracious living, all of which were considered to be among the prime virtues of the 'perfect'

Sir John Wynn of Gwydir. (Engraving by Robert Vaughan.) (*Source: National Museum of Wales.*)

A.16 gentleman (A.16).

The shire community as a self-contained organic entity had also emerged as well as the shiretown where a number of leading gentry began to build new residences for themselves. George Owen, writing in typically eulogistic style in the last decade of the sixteenth century, revelled in the 'joyful metamorphosis' (as he called it) that had occurred in the country's material circumstances, and he portrayed it as having become, by that time, a far more prosperous land than it had been at the turn of
A.17 the century (A.17). In his view it had virtually been born anew in consequence of Henry Tudor's advent to the throne and his son's reforms of government and administration.

The support granted by the Welsh gentry to the Tudor dynasty was reinforced by the loyalty shown to its institutions. They increasingly identified themselves with government and administration and, in a broader perspective, they nurtured an allegiance and a way of life which proved to be nothing but
A.18 beneficial to them (A.18). Their social and economic affairs as well as their official responsibilities were inextricably bound up with a world which often had its power-source located beyond the confines of their respective communities — at Ludlow or London or elsewhere on a far-distant estate. Although Sir William Maurice and his equals found it easy to accept the Stuart succession in 1603 on the grounds that it served to unite the 'ancient empire' of the Britons under one Crown and recognized that Welshmen had their proper role to play in national affairs, he was equally aware of the perils which beset the rural Welsh countryside and the detrimental effects which social trends among the upper gentry would have on the cultural scene. He was obliged on one occasion to reprimand an acquaintance for commenting so disparagingly on the quality of the *bards* and to urge him to speak but the best of his own country. His response explained much about the condition of the Welsh *bardic* tradition, with its 'flaterous' eulogy, at that crucial time but it equally exposed the changing attitudes of most of the upper
A.19 gentry towards their native culture (A.19). With the gradual broadening of their interests and concerns it was only to be expected that in time the majority would withdraw their *bardic* patronage and place less value on conventional pane-

A.20 gyrics (A.20). Doubtless the social effects of the Tudor Settlement did contribute significantly to this ill-fated malaise but it must also be set firmly against a much broader background or pattern of social change and higher material standards of living as well as the bitter effects of economic inflation and allied problems.

Owing to the new and exciting involvement in educational activities and the opportunites which lured ambitious gentry over *Offa's Dyke*, together with the decaying standards of a medieval cultural order unable to compete in the dynamic world of the Renaissance, the old gentry structure began to change significantly. It was in such spirited and self-assured men that the Crown placed entire confidence. Well could William Vaughan of Llangyndeyrn in Carmarthenshire ecstatically recall that *Offa's Dyke* had been 'extinguished with love and charity' and urge both nations 'to dwell together without enmity, without detraction'. Nevertheless, in spite of their pretensions, the Welsh gentry at the close of the sixteenth century still displayed several important vestiges of their Welsh character which often became a source of amusement to their English acquaintances. Social and political circumstances in the succeeding century, however, were to have significant consequences for these natural leaders in the Welsh county communities.

## Notes

1 Thomas Smith, *De Republica Anglorum*, ed. L. Alston, Cambridge, 1906, pp.32-40.

## Sources

A.1 Sir Richard Bulkeley of Beaumaris, Knight . . . was a goodly person fair of complexion and tall of stature . . . He was temperate in his diet, not using tobacco or drinking of healths . . . He never changed his fashion but always wore round breeches and thick bumbast doublets though very gallant and rich. Being demanded why he followed not the fashion his answer was that people were given so much variety and change that once in every seven years they would turn to his fashion . . . He was no great scholar, but a great reader of history and discourses of all estates and countries. Of very good memory and understanding in matters belonging to housekeeping, husbandry, maritime affairs, building of ships and maintaining them at sea. He was so singular in his conceit that he always drew his own letters and answered all letters with his own hand . . . He was a great housekeeper and entertainer of noblemen . . . and strangers, especially such as passed to or from Ireland. He made a great entertainment . . . [and] . . . sent yearly a ship or two to Greenland for Cod, Ling and other fish which he did use to barter in Spain for Malaga and sherry wines . . . His estate in Anglesey was worth 2500 li per annum, in Caernarfonshire 800 li and in Cheshire 100 li, having always a great stock of ready money lying in his chest . . . He kept many servants and attendants, tall and proper men; two lackeys in livery always ran by his horse; he never went from home without 20 or 24 to attend him. He was a great favourite of Queen Elizabeth. He had powerful friends at Court, and had the gentry and commonalty of the country at his service . . . In his latter days he built the house of Baron Hill for the entertainment of Henry, Prince of Wales in his way to Ireland . . .

(*History of the Bulkeley Family* by William Williams of Beaumaris, 1674. National Library of Wales MS 908E. Transcribed in E.G. Jones (ed.), 'History of the Bulkeley Family', *Transaction of the Anglesey Society and Field Club*, 1948, pp.20–1).

A.2 But to return to the offspring of Gruffudd ap Caradog of whose succession with the state and condition they lived in from time to time, being my purpose to entreat of the three brethren Dafydd, Maredudd and Hywel . . . the posterity only of Hywel doth remain in credit and show in their country, the posterity of the other two being by the division and sub-division of *gavelkind* (the destruction of Wales) brought to the estate of mean freeholders, and so having forgotten their descent and pedigree are become as if they never had been. If you ask the question why the succession of Hywel sped better than the posterity of the other two brethren I can yield you no other reason but God's mercy and goodness towards the one more than the other, as God said in the Book of Moses (I will have mercy on whom I will have mercy), for they lived in the same Commonwealth and under the same storm of oppression so as if God had not left us a seed we had been like

Sodom or compared to Gomorra. Nevertheless, by the goodness of God we are and continue in the reputation of gentlemen from time to time sithence unto this day . . . Yet a great temporal blessing it is and a great heart's ease to a man to find that he is well descended, and a greater grief it is for upstarts and gent of the first head to look back unto their descents, being base in such sort, as I have known many such hate gent in their hearts for no other cause but that they were gent.

(Sir John Wynn, *The History of the Gwydir Family*, early seventeenth century, transcribed in J. Ballinger (ed.), *The History of the Gwydir Family*, 1927, pp.14, 36).

A.3 I would I had an hour to speak my mind to you. I think it not expedient to have justices of the peace and gaol delivery in Wales, for there are very few Welsh in Wales above Brecknock who have 10 li. land, and their discretion is less than their land.

(Rowland Lee to Thomas Cromwell, 12 March 1536. *Letters and Papers*, Henry VIII, vol.X, no.453, p.182).

A.4 For now the poor tenant . . . is taught to sing unto his lord a new song, and the landlords have learnt the text of the damned disciple, 'quod vultis mihi dare, et ego illum vobis tradam' [What are you willing to give to me and I will betray him to you?]. And now the world is so altered with the poor tenant that he standeth so in bodily fear of his greedy neighbour, that ii or iii years were his lease end, he must bow to his lord for a new lease and must pinch it out many years before to keep money together, so that in his age it is as easy for a poor tenant to marry ii of his daughters to his neighbour's sons as to match himself to a good farm from his landlord.

(George Owen, *The Description of Penbrockshire*, 1603. Transcribed in H. Owen, (ed.), *The Description of Pembrokeshire*, Cymmrodorion Record Series, 1, vol.I, 1892 pp.190–1).

A.5 Maredudd, son to Ieuan ap Robert, his eldest son, in the time of his father was taken to nurse by an honest freeholder in the hundred of Isgwyrfai that was owner of the Crug in Llanfair, and

Map of Pembrokeshire by George Owen of Henllys. (*Source: National Library of Wales.*)

the best man in the parish, and having no children of his own gave his inheritance to his foster-child . . . Crug standeth between Caernarfon and Bangor two miles off from Caernarfon. In those days Caernarfon flourished as well by trade of merchandise . . . the way to London and to the marches little frequented whereby civility and learning flourished in that town . . . thither did his foster-father send my great-grandfather to school, where to learnt the English tongue, to read, to write and to understand Latin, a matter of great moment in those days . . . At Crug he began the world with his wife . . . then finding he was likely to have more children . . . he did purchase a lease of the castle and *ffriddoedd* of Dolwyddelan . . . Being questioned by his friends what he meant to leave his ancient house and habitation and to go to dwell to Nanconwy swarming with thieves and bondmen (whereof there are many in the king's lordship and towns in that hundred), he answered that he should find elbow room in that waste country among the bondmen, and that he had rather fight with outlaws and thieves than with his own blood and kindred . . . To strengthen himself in the country he provided out of all countries adjacent the tallest and most able men he could hear of. Of them he placed colonies in the country filling every empty tenement with a tenant or two whereof most was the king's land . . .

(Sir John Wynn, *The History of the Gwydir Family*, early seventeenth century. Ballinger, op.cit., pp.50–1, 54).

A.6 To the Right Honourable the Lord President and others etc . . . Whereas most of the land in these two counties consists of mountains, hills and other waste ground on which the freeholders have had as far back as can be remembered Common of Pasture all the year round, so breeding yearly great numbers of horses, mares and geldings as well for the maintenance of the strength of the Realm as for the upkeep of tillage; also no small number of oxen, kine, sheep and other cattle for food. Yet divers persons within these counties, preferring their private lucre and gain before the welfare of their country, have within the last twenty years or so acquired cottages and other small freeholds and do in the summer put on the mountains and hills not only their own cattle (which they keep elsewhere than upon their lands in these counties in winter) but also cattle hired from other men, making such number of cattle as the hill pasture will scarce suffice to feed for half the summer. As a result the commons are left so barren that your orators' cattle die yearly in the winter to the great hindrance of the commonwealth not only of the inhabitants of these counties but also of those near adjoining.

(Petition by Edward Herbert and James Price Esqs. and other freeholders of Montgomeryshire and Radnorshire to the Council in the Marches, *c.*1573, transcribed in R. Flenley (ed.), *A Calendar of the Register of the Council in the Marches of Wales, 1509–1591*, Cymmrodorion Record Series, 1916, pp.105–6).

A.7 A Schedule Indented Containing what goods and chattels, movables Edward Jones of Cadwgan in the County of Denbigh, esquire, lately attainted, was possessed of the Vth day of June anno Regni Regine Elizabeth xxviii and at other times after before his death viz.

Imprimis in the hall of the mansion house of the said Edward Jones called Plas Cadwgan i drawing table of ash, i form of joiner's work, i other table with two forms, i little table at the screen, i standing cupboard of wainscot valued at xxvii s vii d

Item in the little parlour adjoining to the hall one square table of walnut tree, ii forms to the same, i Flanders chair, i low stool for a woman and ii stools of walnut tree valued at xv s

Item in the little buttery or pantry, i bin for bread, i coffer cupboard wise, i cupboard and iii shelves valued at vi s vii d

Item in the cellar ii joists to set on beer, i tub to salt beef in, iiii barrels for beer, i chest to put candles in, and two hanging shelves valued at x s

Item in the great parlour on the north end of the hall, i drawing table of walnut, iii stools, i court cupboard, i little square table, and i iron hearth graven in the back of the chimney valued at iii li

Item in the kitchen one table, ii forms ii dressing tables about the kitchen, ii kettles, i little pan, i pot with pothooks, i bar of iron to hang the pot on, ii gobarts, ii spits, i skillet, vii old pewter dishes, i frying pan, i dripping pan, ii candlesticks, vii saucers, i plate of pewter and i old pipe of lead valued at xl s

Item in the chamber called Edward Jones's own bed chamber i bedstead of wainscot, one featherbed, i blanket, i covering, i bolster, i pillow with curtains of green flannel, i cupboard, i square table, ii joined stools, iii chests whereof ii Flanders and i dansk, ii curtains, and ii rods of iron, xiii pairs of sheets whereof iiii pair flaxen, one dozen and a half napkins, iii towels, v tablecloths whereof iii flaxen and iiii pillowberes valued at viii li

(An Inventory of furniture at Plas Cadwgan in 1586). P.R.O. Exchequer Special Proceedings (Denbs.), no. 3400. Transcribed in E.G. Jones (ed.), 'Plas Cadwgan in 1586', *Transactions of the Denbighshire Historical Society*, vol.6, 1957, pp.13–15).

A.8 Loving cousin. After my right hearty commendations I being yet unacquainted with you, have in the behalf of Walter Vaughan my son been a suitor unto you by my nephew Hugh ap Hugh, who repaired unto you and was kindly entertained and welcome, for the which I yield you thanks now. If it please you to communicate or talk further with us in this matter, upon the good answer which I have received from you, both I and my son will travel up for I have no other but him only to bestow such living as God hath sent me after my decease which shall be a thousand marks by the year at the least. Beseeching you to continue your good will and forwardness herein as I understand you have begun, which by God's grace shall not on my part and my son's be unacquitted. And thus leaving all to your good discretion to be conferred with my cousin Hugh ap Hugh I commit you to the governance of Almighty God. From my house at Gelli Aur the vith day of April 1571.

Your assured cousin
John Vaughan

(J. Ballinger (ed.), *Calendar of Wynn of Gwydir Papers*, 1926, no.43. Transcribed in J. Ballinger, 'Katheryn of Berain', *Y Cymmrodor*, XI, 1929, p.12).

A.9 Robert Wynn, born at Gwydir . . . third son to John Wynn ap Maredudd, serving Sir Philip Hoby, Knight, in his Chamber, being one of ye Council of King Henry ye 8 and a great Commander of his army, was with ye king and his master at ye

Siege of Boulogne where he received a shot in his leg whereof he was long lame . . . First he married Dorothy [daughter] of Sir William Gruffudd of Penrhyn, Knight, Chamberlain of North Wales and widow to William Williams ye younger of Cochwilan, Esqr . . . after he marries a young gentlewoman, daughter of Thomas Dymock of Wellington in ye county of Flint Esqr . . . he was at ye winning and burning of Edinburgh and Leith in Scotland and at ye memorable journeys mentioned in ye chronicles in King Henry ye 8 and Edward ye 6 time . . . His master was sent ambassador to ye Emperor Charles ye 5th who was then in Hungary with the greatest army that the Christians ever had to confront. Suleiman the Turk that came with 500,000 thousand men to conquer Christendom at which service both his master and he was . . . Robert Wynn . . . returned home . . . and built a goodly house in ye town of Conwy . . . where he kept a worthy plentiful house all his time and lieth buried in ye church there . . .

(Sir John Wynn, *The History of the Gwydir Family*, early seventeenth century. Ballinger, op.cit., pp.69–71).

A.10 But sithence the time of Henry 7 and Henry 8 that we were emancipated as it were and made free to trade and traffic through England, the gentlemen and people in Wales have greatly increased in learning and civility for now great numbers of youths are continuely brought up and maintained at the universities of Oxford and Cambridge and in other good schools in England where some prove to be learned men and good members in the Commonwealth of England and Wales; some worthy labourers in the Lord's vineyard, many of them have proved excellent in ye Civil Laws, some in Physick and other laudable studies wherein they are found nothing behind other nations; many good grammar schools in divers parts of the country are now to be found throughout Wales whereby the country is grown and shortly like to be as civil as any other place of this land . . . No country in England so flourished in one hundred years as Wales hath done sithence the government of Henry 7 to this time . . . the people changed in heart within and the land altered in hue without, from evil to good and from bad to better . . .

(George Owen, *The Dialogue of the Government of Wales*, 1594, in H. Owen (ed.), *The History of Pembrokeshire*, Cymmr. Records Series, I, 1982, vol.III, p.56).

A.11 Therefore praise God that thou hast careful parents to place thee in Oxford, a famous university, the fountain and well-head of all learning. Keep company with honest students who abhore evil courses as drinking and taking tobacco to their own loss and discredit of their friends and parents who sent them to the university for better purposes . . . I will allow you no servitor, You may serve yourself and spare 6d a week. Take heed lest you be guiled by the butler that he set down in his book more for bread and beer than you call for. Speak no Welsh to any that can speak English, no not to your bedfellows, and thereby you may . . . freely speak English tongue perfectly. I had rather that you should keep company with studious, honest Englishmen than with many of your own countrymen who are more prone to be idle and riotous than the English.

(William Wynn of Glyn, Merioneth to his son Cadwaladr at Oxford, no date. Transcribed in T. Jones Pierce (ed.), 'Calendar of the Clenennau Letters and Papers in the Brogyntyn Collection', *National Library of Wales Journal*, Supp. Series IV, Pt.1, 1947, pp.126–7).

A.12 I am well afraid if ye knew their demeanours in their country ye would not be contented with them, for their father and friend have been always against them that be newers in their parties, and have imagined disorder and murder, and within this xii months have set upon my Lord Deputy there, and murdered his servant and maimed ii or iii more of his servants at the king's castle at Cardiff; and there is of them xii brothers and the most part bastards, and have no living but by extortion and pilling of the king's subjects.

(Elizabeth, Countess of Worcester to Thomas Cromwell concerning Thomas and Henry Stradling, 1533. B.M. Cottonian Collection; Vespasian F, XIII, F.180. Transcribed by G.E.

Jones, 'Local Administration and Justice in Glamorgan', *Morgannwg*, IX, 1965, pp.28–9).

A.13 The great disorders in Wales especially in South Wales have grown much of late days, by retainers of gentlemen whom they must after the manner of the country bear out in all actions be they never so bad.

They have also foster brothers loitering and idle kinsmen, and other hangers on that do nothing else but play at cards and dice and pick and steal and kill or hurt any man when they will have them and yet they themselves will wash their hands thereof when the ill fact is done. These idle loiterers when they have offended will be shifted off to some friends of theirs in another quarter so as they will not be found to be punished when time shall require, and in the meanwhile the gentlemen will practise an agreement with the parties grieved and then because the loiterers have nothing of their own, the gentlemen must help them to a *cymortha* to satisfy the parties damnified . . . Contempts and disorders must be severely punished and the better the man offender the greater the offence and the punishment ought to be the more which must be rather the body by imprisonment than in purse lest the country by *cymortha* bear that pain more than the offender.

(Dr David Lewis: part of his information on the disorders of Wales, 1575. Transcribed in D.Ll. Thomas, 'Further Notes on the Council in the Marches', App.C, *Y Cymmrodor*, XIII, 1899).

A.14 You will find some men that, so soon as they see the river Severn, or the steeples of Shrewsbury, and hear the Englishman but once say 'Good Morrow', they shall begin to put their Welsh out of mind and to speak it in most corrupt fashion. Their Welsh will be of an English cut, and their English (God knows) too much after the Welsh fashion. And this cometh either of very foolishness or of a saucy pride and vanity. For he is never seen for a kindly, virtuous man that will deny whether it be his father, or his mother, or his country or his tongue.

(Gruffudd Robert's comment on the anglicizing influences on the Welsh gentry, 1567. Free translation in H.I. Bell, *A History of*

*Welsh Literature*, Clarendon, 1955. Translation of T. Parry, *Hanes Llenyddiaeth Gymraeg*, p.211).

A.15 To Edward Stradling, Welshman, gilded knight and illustrious man outstanding for his learning and wisdom, an excellent patron of letters and man of letters.

Illustrious and high-born knight! I recall how once I came to visit you and your most noble wife at celebrated St Donat's Castle — your ancient seat, and that of your ancestors, knights renowned for their rank — and how I chanced there upon a charming poem . . . composed in Latin metres, and in it . . . the poet extolled the site of that well-fortified castle, by far the most agreeable site anywhere. Furthermore, he praised those costly structures, whose material had almost all been extracted by you from the very sea's rocks at great expense, structures which you raised on the furthermost edge of the shore in a wonderful manner . . . You are a man who are most happily versed in letters, and are so fashioned by the charm which attaches to them that your home is always open to all men of learning. For you find your pleasure in joining in discussion with such men, you exercise your own genius as you delight in talking to them, and thus you summon back the vigour of your tired mind. Furthermore, not only have you stayed for a long time in Italy . . . but you have also travelled the greater part of the rest of Europe. The result of all this is that experience has produced learning in you, and learning so many virtues.

(Sion Dafydd Rhys's letter to Sir Edward Stradling of St Donat's, 1592, in C. Davies, *Latin Writers of the Renaiisance*, Cardiff, 1981, pp.6–7, 10).

A.16

There we have had you, every man seeks you,
As I prophesied in song . . .
There never was better in power,
In horses and men, a better knight . . .
Thy court where alms are given
Thither wend young and old . . .
It was a lodging for the whole of Wales . . .
Many a feast for earls, lords

Of double estate, in thy mansion,
Many a fair course from thy kitchen
And the wild flow of tuns of wine . . .

(Sion Tudur: ode to Sir Thomas Mostyn of Mostyn, 1599, in E.D. Jones, 'The Brogyntyn Welsh Manuscripts', *National Library of Wales Journal*, VI, Summer, 1949, p.23. Free translation).

A.17 Whereby the people are grown to be of great wealth, the gentlemen of great livings, so that in a country, when it come first to be shire-ground, where there was scarce two gentlemen that could in lands dispend twenty pounds apiece, there are now in the said shire to be found some that doth receive yearly five hundred pounds, some three hundred pounds, and many one hundred pounds good lands, so that now there is no shire in Wales but is able to yield sufficient numbers of gentlemen that may dispend 100 pounds a year good land . . . Now we see the old castles of Wales from whence in old time issued out daily our destroyers and disinheritors, all in ruin and decay, and on the contrary the houses of the gentlemen and people to flourish and increase which were most commonly burnt once every year in times past. This is a joyful metamorphosis for Wales . . .

(George Owen, *The Dialogue of the Government of Wales*, 1594. H. Owen, op.cit., vol.III, p.57).

A.18 . . . at which time all Wales was restored inheritable to the laws of England . . . whereby all Wales was divided into twelve shires or counties . . . for which benefit all the country of Wales is bound to make earnest prayer unto Almighty God long to preserve his posterity to reign over them in continual felicity . . .

This alteration of government is worthy of remembrance as well for the singular commodity the inhabitants of Wales receive thereby as the commonwealth universally . . .

Now, since Wales was thus, by gracious King Henry VIII, enabled with the laws of England, and thereby united to the same, and so brought to a monarchy, which is the most sure, stable and best regiment, they are exempted from the dangers before remembered; for now life and death, lands and goods rest in this monarchy, and not in the pleasure of the subject . . . The discord between England and Wales, then, procured slaughters, invasions, enmities, burnings, poverty and such like fruits of war. This unity engendered friendship, amity, love, alliance . . . assistance, wealth and quietness. God preserve and increase it.

(Rhys Meurig of Cottrel, *Morganiae Archaiographia*, 1578, in B.Ll. James (ed.), *Morganiae Archaiographia*, South Wales Record Society, vol.I, 1983, pp.67–8).

A.19

To versify with flattering tongue
Men's pedigrees, is that not wrong? . . .
To mean and strengthless men to give
Such praise as warriors might receive;
Breeding and noble bounty see,
With endless hospitality.
In one within whose mansion's bound
Neither bed nor board is found,
Merit and honour to ascribe,
Fond hope, to the worthless for a bribe,
And boldly claim, by the same rule,
Wisdom for the veriest fool.

(Edmwnd Prys: satire on the *bardic order*, *c.*1580. Free translation in H.I. Bell, op.cit., p.207).

A.20 He would be counted a *bard* and a poet . . . Of his skill in poetry I am not able to judge, but I can tell you for a truth how old William Basset of Bewper, a good learned esqr judged of it, who was a man very judicial indeed. This *bard* resorting abroad to gentlemen's houses in the loitering time between Christmas and Candlemas to sing songs and receive rewards, coming to Bewper he presented the good old squire with a *cywydd*, *ode* or *englyn* (I know not whither) containing partly the praises of the gentleman, and partly the pedigrees and matches of his ancestors. The gentleman, having perused the rhyme, prepared in his hand a noble for a reward and called the poet who came with a good will; of whom he demanded whether he had

Beaupré Castle, home of the Basset family of Beaupré (or Bewper). (*Source: National Monuments Record for Wales.*)

reserved to himself any copy of that rhyme; no by my faith (said the rhymer) but I hope to take a copy of that which I delivered you. Then replied the gentleman, hold, here is thy fee, and by my honesty I swear if there be no copy of this extant, none shall there ever be, and therewith put it sure enough into the fire.

(An extract from Sir John Stradling's account of the dispute over the burrows of Merthyr Mawr, *c.*1600. H.J. Randall and W. Rees (eds.), 'The Story of the Lower Burrows of Merthyr Mawr (Sir John Stradling)', *South Wales and Monmouthshire Record Society Publications*, I, 1932, pp.70–1).

## Debating the Evidence

Much of the past is completely closed to us. There are uncountable numbers of people and events, even in our own country's past, whom we can never know about, let alone begin to consider their motives, emotions and thoughts. The study of history has to be the study of what *remains* of the past, the buildings, the artefacts, the documents, the tape recordings. All the historian can do in his attempt to interpret that past is to squeeze as much information out of what remains as possible. He is constrained at all times by the limits of the *evidence*.

As a general rule, though this is not invariably the case, the further back we go in the past the less evidence there is. For the Tudor period there are far fewer documents about far fewer people than is the case for the nineteenth century, for example. Another general constraint is that there is far more information available for the higher ranks in society than for the lower. Monarchs and prime ministers generate a lot more paper about themselves and tend to live in more permanent buildings than do barrow boys. As a result we know much more about Tudor gentlemen than we do about Tudor labourers. However, the evidence is still relatively sparse for the lives of the Welsh gentry. Gwynfor Jones's essay draws on some of the most important types of written evidence which survive from the period — contemporary or near-contemporary accounts written by or about gentry families, correspondence and inventories of possessions. The most intriguing sources he uses are the poems.

*Source A.1*

1. One of the most significant things about this document, as in any document, is its date. Does the date of this document make it a primary or secondary source for the history of Tudor Wales?

2. Sir Richard Bulkeley died in 1621. He was head of a particularly important gentry family in Beaumaris, Anglesey. Where might William Williams have obtained his information?

3. One of the problems of making sense of any historical document is the specialist vocabulary used. There are no esoteric legal or administrative terms used here, so why does this difficulty of interpretation arise?

4. What bias might there be in this document?

*Source A.2*

How far would you trust the social analysis in this document? What does the document tell us about Tudor views on gentility? Why do you think gentry like Sir John Wynn were concerned with topics like heraldry and genealogy?

*Source A.3*

What is there in this document which might indicate that Rowland Lee was a particularly biased commentator? In what way might the document tell us something of the economic condition of Wales compared with that of England? Why might Lee make a distinction between gentry south of Brecon and those north of Brecon?

*Source A.4*

*George Owen* was the sixteenth-century head of a gentry family with a large estate at Henllys, Pembrokeshire [Dyfed]. His forbears had built up the Henllys estate slowly and painstakingly, so that by 1497 Rhys ap Owain Fychan, *George Owen*'s grandfather, was already designated 'gentleman'. *George Owen*'s father was at various times mayor of Pembroke and controller of the ports of Pembroke, Haverfordwest and Tenby. What kinds of viewpoint might you expect *George Owen* to have? Are your preconceptions borne out by this document? What sort of economic circumstances might produce shorter leases?

*Source A.6*

Edward Herbert and James Price are 'esquires'. They had not achieved the highest gentry status of knighthood but they were the next rank of gentry. In the light of this information how far do you trust this appeal to the *Council in the Marches*? What is being demonstrated in this document is a clash between the ancient communal claims to pasture of poorer tenant farmers and the ambitions of new estate-building gentry. How far does the evidence of exploitation of higher ground point to the same thing?

*Source A.7*

An inventory of this kind would seem to be the sort of evidence which is completely reliable. Are there any reasons why it might not be so? What more information would it be useful to have before using this document? On the basis of this inventory what sort of picture do we get of the life of a minor gentleman? In what ways would a well equipped museum of the Tudor period provide better evidence?

*Source A.8*

What unfamiliar terms would you need to define before making full use of this letter? Katheryn of Berain (*c.*1534–91) was one of the most remarkable of Tudor ladies. She was renowned for her wealth and beauty and was married four times. Her first marriage was to John Salesbury and after his death she married Sir Richard Clough of Denbigh, a very rich merchant who settled with his wife in Antwerp. After his death she married Maurice Wynn of Gwydir and, finally, Edward Thelwall. All her husbands were members of rich gentry families. In the light of this, what does the letter tell us of marriage etiquette and the social significance of Tudor marriages?

*Source A.9*

Sir John Wynn was head, in Elizabeth's time, of a particularly important gentry family in north Wales, the Wynns of Gwydir. From this document what information would you be able to glean as to what he thought important in his own family's history? The dots are a standard form of indicating that the author has left sections out of the document. Why might he have done this? What implications does this have for our understanding of the document?

*Source A.10*

*George Owen* helped greatly to establish a new orthodoxy about the beneficence of Tudor rule in Wales and about the advance in 'civility' in the country in the sixteenth century. How far did his own birth, position and career shape his views?

*Source A.11*

Do passages such as these confirm the view that linguistic and cultural uniformity was as much a gentry aspiration within Wales as the view that they were imposed on Wales by legislation?

*Source A.12*

There is transparent bias in this source, but what view of the nature of social dominance and the way in which local power was exercised does it give us? When you have read the essays by Glanmor Williams and Penry Williams examine the question again.

*Source A.13*

Compare this evidence with that in Source A.12. Do they corroborate each other? (*Cymortha* was a forced payment by lords on tenants, a distortion of the community aid of medieval Wales).

*Source A.14*

Gruffudd Robert (*c.*1522–*c.*1610) was an important and staunch Roman Catholic, influential in Mary's reign as Archdeacon of Anglesey, who chose exile rather than stay in England in Elizabeth's reign. His writings in Welsh were essential to the Catholic counter-reformation. Compare and contrast Gruffudd Robert's attitude to that of William Wynn in Source A.11. What do these sources tell us about the attitude of influential Welshmen to things English?

*Source A.15*

From this letter can you guess what the relationship between Sion Dafydd Rhys and Sir Edward Stradling was? What does this passage tell us of the way in which cultural influences from Europe might reach Wales? And what does it reveal of the attitude of English gentry families in Wales towards native culture?

*Source A.16*
What might be the strengths and weaknesses of poetry as a historical source?

*Source A.17*
Compare this with the comments in A.3. Can *George Owen*'s comments be borne out by considering the evidence of architecture, for example the decay of castles or the building of country residences?

*Source A.18*
What view of government and its contribution to social peace did *Rice Merrick*, or Rhys Meurig, hold?

*Source A.19*
Does what you read here affect your view of Source A.16?

*Source A.20*
From this source, and Sources A.16 and A.19, assess the relationship between *bards* and gentry in Tudor Welsh society.

## Discussion

There is an interesting problem in the nature of the evidence about the Tudor gentry which poses particular problems for the historian. As we mentioned in the introduction, there is far more evidence about them than there is for those lower down the social scale. The paradox is that most of the documents cited here are written by the gentry themselves. They were the literate members of society. They were particularly interested in the history of their own families and tended to write about them. They were at the centre of local government and tended to correspond with each other. Our three major informants in these documents, Sir John Wynn of Gwydir, *Rice Merrick* of Cottrell, and *George Owen* of Henllys, were all gentry. Inevitably, therefore, their analyses will reflect the concerns and attitudes of their own class. When, for example, in Document A.2, Sir John Wynn comments on how important it is for gentry to be 'well descended', that is to come from an ancient and socially superior family, it is likely that this is an attitude which will be shared by his fellow gentry. When we look for corroboration of this attitude in other gentry writings they are easy to find. We can safely say that coming from an ancient family was of material assistance in being recognized as a gentleman — though it was by no means the only factor.

When, in Document A.17, *George Owen* deals with the transformation which has come over Wales with the advent of the Tudors, we are on more difficult ground. Obviously *George Owen* himself believed that the gentry as a class had grown more prosperous (compare Document A.3). He also believed that the government of Wales had improved out of all recognition as a result of the accession of Henry VII and the legislation of Henry VIII's reign (Document A.10). How far is this reliable evidence? *Was* there such a transformation? Certainly there is something in what *Owen* says. The old castles of Wales were no longer the defensive fortresses which had once had to resist regular Welsh rebellions against their Norman conquerors. Tudor gentry could safely convert some of these buildings into commodious homes with imposing Tudor windows as did Sir John Perrott in Carew, or Sir Edward Stradling in St Donat's. And yet, if we look at Document A.3, we get a different picture of the Welsh gentry. It could, of course, be that the discrepancy in the dates accounts for this. But if we look at Document A.14, the picture which emerges is certainly not of a society which has experienced a transition from lawlessness to tranquility. Part of the answer must be that *George Owen* is, perhaps without realizing it, representing the attitude of that class of people, the gentry, who had done so well out of the Tudor settlement. This topic is more fully discussed in Section E, but it is important to note that we do not get an unbiased view from *George Owen*. The status and background of the writer is an essential element in assessing the reliability of the information.

Another issue dealt with in the sources is the reaction of the gentry to things English, especially language and education. Here we have documents emanating from gentry who thoroughly support increased contact with the English and their language and education (A.10 and A.11) and someone who opposes it (A.14). When writers looking at the evidence from opposite sides seem to agree on the facts there is likely to be much truth in those facts. The gentry did enjoy the new opportunities which union with England offered them. The documents can not answer the question whether this was something to be applauded or criticized.

# *The Lower Orders*

BRIAN HOWELLS

It is generally agreed by historians that the most significant social division in Tudor society was that between the nobility and gentry on the one hand and, on the other, the 'non-gentle' elements in society, the lower orders, comprising at least 95 per cent of the population. Most people in the latter grouping were peasants, smallholders whose view of the world was moulded by the traditional cultures of their local communities and who relied upon farming as their principal means of subsistence. Their lives were hard and their economic difficulties increased markedly during the period in which the Tudors sat on the throne. When Henry Tudor became King, Wales, like England, had not yet recovered from the effect of the great population slump which had occurred in the late middle ages. *Villeinage* had virtually disappeared, labourers and small farmers were enjoying a relatively high standard of living, and so slack was the demand for land that rents were low and some holdings unoccupied for want of tenants. Within a couple of generations, however, the situation had
B.1 changed drastically (B.1). There was a dramatic increase in population which resulted in severe inflation, the prices of some foodstuffs increasing sixfold during the course of the sixteenth century, land hunger, a substantial increase in the proportion of landless people in society, a labour glut, and relatively low wages. Many peasants also found that, because land was becoming a more valuable commodity, they were subjected to determined attempts to oust them from their farmlands or to increase their rents.

For them it was, as *George Owen* remarked, 'a new world', and one in which perhaps the most important single feature affecting

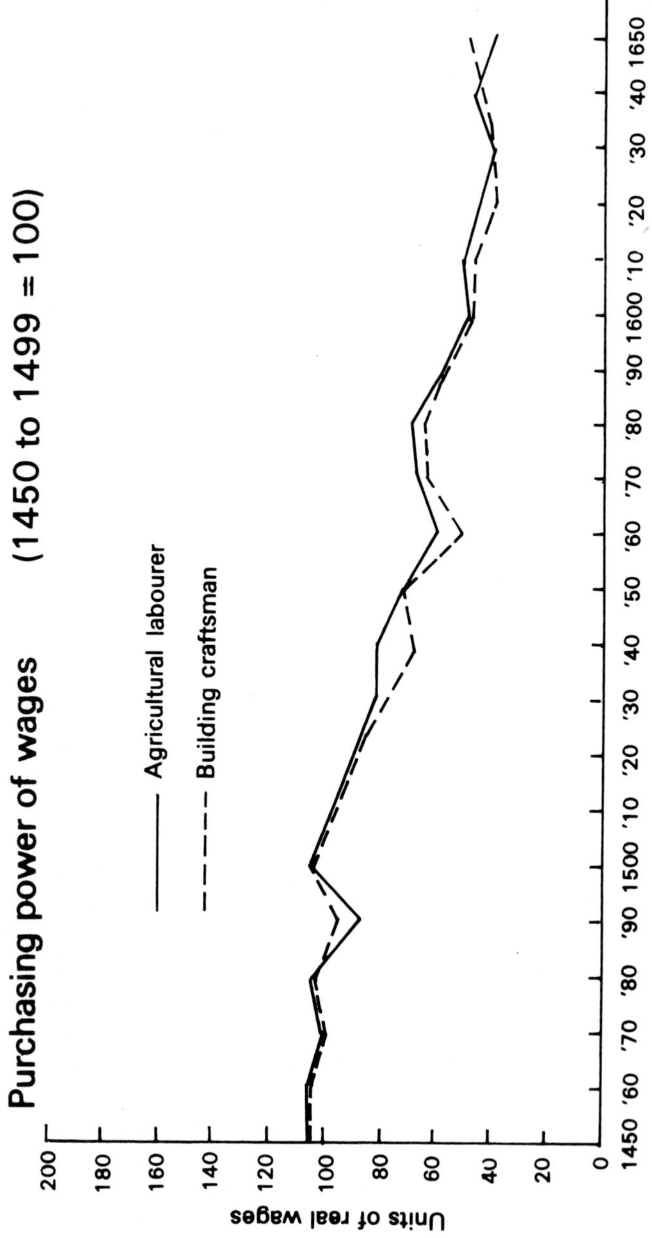
Purchasing power of wages (1450 to 1499 = 100)
Agricultural labourer
Building craftsman
Units of real wages
200
180
160
140
120
100
80
60
40
20
0
1450 '60 '70 '80 '90 1500 '10 '20 '30 '40 '50 '60 '70 '80 '90 1600 '10 '20 '30 '40 1650

the welfare of the peasant was the terms upon which he held his land, for these determined the length and security of his tenancy, the amount of profit which was creamed off by his landlord, and whether or not his widow and heir could retain the family farm after his death. Terminal conditions varied everywhere, their complexities and uncertainties providing a field day for the lawyers. Ensnared by intimidation and the expense of litigation, many peasant farmers failed to defend themselves adequately in the crown courts and in consequence lost some or all of their lands, but the courts were inclined to extend their protection to peasant tenants whenever it could be proved that the *custom of the manor* favoured their case. Manorial customary law was promulgated constantly in the manorial courts, passed on carefully from one generation of tenants to the next, and often written down in manorial surveys and *custumals*. It was of critical importance to tenants insofar as it affected the holding and devolution of their lands. Most secure of all tenants were freeholders, who often paid only nominal rents, and those tenants, holding mostly old *villein and escheat lands*, whose rents and entry fines (the sums of money payable when they took up their tenancies) were fixed by manorial custom. Frequently, however, *manorial custom* did not give protection to peasant farmers. There were many whose rents and entry fines were not fixed by custom and who could never be sure that their dependants would be able to retain the land after their deaths, whilst most vulnerable of all were those who held land by one-year leases: from the mid-sixteenth century such unfortunates came under increasing pressure both from landlords seeking to increase their incomes and from the competition of other land-hungry peasants.

These and other major changes created serious tensions within Tudor society. What held it together, more than anything else, was general acceptance of the ancient view that people should accept unquestioningly the validity of the existing social hierarchy, discharge the responsibilities and exercise the privileges appropriate to the status to which they had been born, and obey their social superiors. According to this theory, the sacred right to rule had been conferred by God upon the monarch, who in turn devolved it upon those through whom the realm was governed: at

the lowest levels of society this authority would be exercised by the father over his family, and by the master over his work-
B.2 force (B.2). To challenge it was, as churchmen stressed, a form of sacrilege which merited condign punishment. At every level, social status was reflected in outward appearance, lifestyle and responsibilities, and even within the non-gentle sector of society there were generally-recognized social divisions. Thus the peasantry, comprising the great majority of Tudor Welshmen, was regarded by contemporaries as embracing a number of distinct socio-economic groupings — substantial farmers or *yeomen*, farmers of small and middling means know as *husbandmen*, the labouring classes and, at the bottom of the social scale, the
B.3 paupers (B.3).

Social categorizing has its difficulties, not least those stemming from the fact that various groups tended to overlap. The Tudor gentry clearly regarded themselves as distinct from, and socially superior to, *yeomen*, but many Welsh *yeomen* were descended from *cadet* branches of gentry families, and it was not uncommon for them to be wealthier than the poorer gentry. Moreover, the *yeomen* and lesser gentry shared similar roles in public affairs, taking their turns on *hundredal juries* and on the petty and sometimes the grand juries of *quarter and great sessions*, attending county courts and participating in elections for knights of the shire, serving as high constables of *hundreds*, and working side by side in ordering the affairs of the localities in which they lived. There were parts of Wales in which, by the late sixteenth century, many *yeomen* were literate, but it is impossible without further research to know how widespread literacy was at this level. Like the *Kulaks* of pre-Revolutionary Russia, they formed a self-conscious status group set apart from the rest of the peasantry by virtue of wealth, their scale of living, and the sizes of their farms. Indeed, in many areas there were clearly-recognized '*yeomen farms*' just as there were recognizable gentry estates. For the most part these were ancient freeholds, but there were *yeomen* who farmed mainly *leasehold* and customary lands. If there was no resident gentry family in the parish the *yeomen* would provide social leadership, holding the most important parochial offices and serving as overseers of the poor, surveyors of highways and churchwardens.

They constituted the most stable element in peasant society. In the Elizabethan period many seem to have rebuilt or modernized their farmhouses. Instead of living in a large, dimly-lit hall with a hearth in the middle of the floor and the smoke escaping eventually through a louvre in the roof, the new vogue with the go-ahead yeoman was for a two-storeyed house with a larger number of rooms, purpose-built chimneys, staircases giving easy access to the upper rooms, and small windows fitted usually with semi-opaque materials but occasionally with glass. It all made for a considerable advance in terms of comfort and privacy, and it is clear from the *probate* inventories of *yeomen* both that their houses were amply furnished and that many flaunted a number of
B.4 prestige possessions such as silver spoons and salt cellars (B.4). Often they kept weapons in their houses, for, like able-bodied men of all other social groups, they were liable to serve in the
B.5 militia (B.5).

Only a small minority of Welsh peasants were *yeomen*: the great majority were *husbandmen*, farmers who occupied small to middling-sized holdings and who, even in good times, could hope
B.6 to achieve only a modest level of prosperity (B.6). Many were materially little better off than labourers and forced to supplement their incomes by working on a part-time or seasonal basis for large farmers or in the woollen, fishing, mining and craft industries. Often it is very difficult to establish precisely how large their farms were, for most manorial rentals and surveys of the period list tenants without revealing the names of the sub-tenants who, in many instances, actually worked the land. It is evident that during Elizabeth's reign most of them farmed smallholdings which were either customary holdings with unfixed rents, unfixed fines, or both, or else lands leased from manorial tenants. This meant that they were at the mercy of their landlords, who could afford to pick and choose their tenants and exact food-gifts and labour services in addition to high cash rents. Furthermore, many lived on such a narrow margin between sufficiency and disaster that in years of cattle disease or crop failure they faced what French historians have termed 'crises of subsistence'.

In early modern England roughly one harvest in six was a failure, and whilst there is no certainty that this was the case in Wales, where patterns of corn production showed considerable

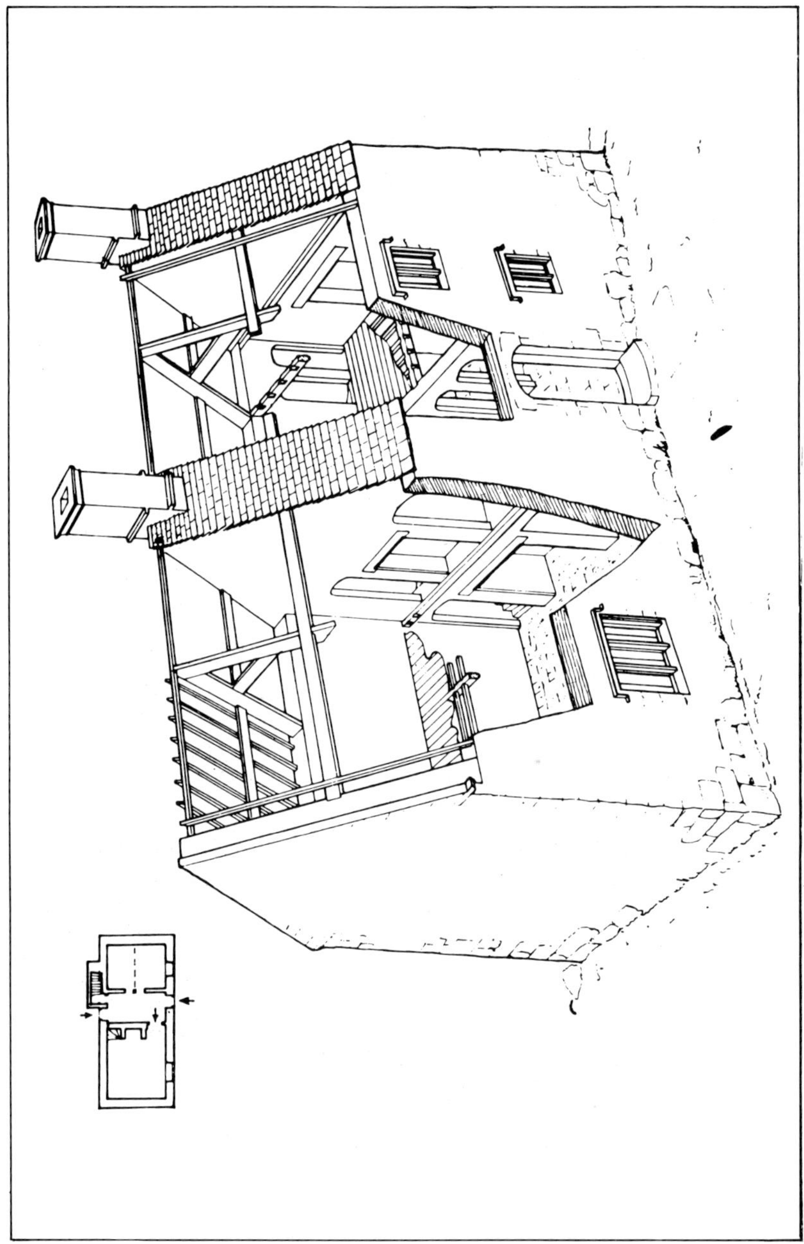

The type of house favoured by south Wales yeomen during the 'great rebuilding'. (*Source: Cambridge University Press.*)

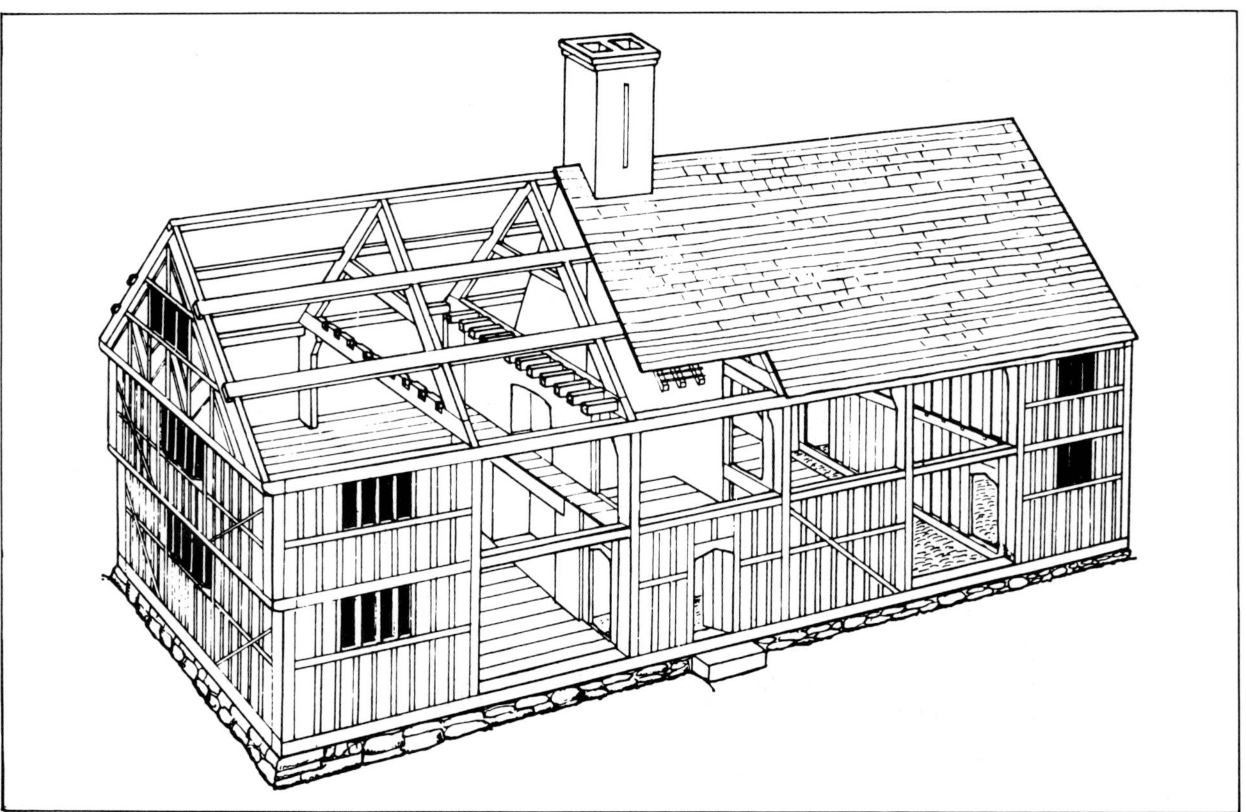

The type of house commonly favoured in the Severn valley during the 'great rebuilding'. (*Source: Cambridge University Press.*)

local variations and defective documentation precludes the construction of grain price indices for most years, the general effects of harvest failure were similar. Even though harvest failure may not have caused widespread starvation in Wales, as was often the case in sixteenth- and seventeenth-century France, it did force many *husbandmen* to face various unpleasant options. Most Welsh farmers, even in upland areas, strove to be as self-reliant as possible in terms of corn production. Because they were not primarily concerned with production for the open market but with supplying their own households, they often grew small acreages of several different grains as part of their mixed farming programmes, thereby minimizing the chances of total crop failure. When harvests were particularly bad, though, they had to choose between borrowing corn or money, selling off some of their livestock, or eating into their seed-corn, thereby jeopardizing the harvest of the following year. Temporary indebtedness was widespread among the *husbandmen* of Tudor Wales, but debt increased radically following catastrophic harvests and outbreaks of disease among livestock, and sometimes led to the borrowing of large sums which could only be secured by mortgaging their lands. The number of unredeemed *mortgages* surviving amongst the estate records of the landed gentry tells its own story.

It would be wrong to represent the *husbandmen* of Tudor Wales
B.7 as being fully self-subsistent (B.7). Normally they tried to produce as many of the necessaries of life as possible themselves, but they were inexorably caught up in a cash economy and one which functioned imperfectly because of periodic shortages of corn in the countryside. Cash had to be found to pay rents and fines, to meet taxes due to the Crown, county rates and parish dues, to make occasional payments to priests and lawyers, and for purchasing goods such as salt, pitch and iron which were normally acquired from the merchants of the market towns. Those who failed to meet their financial obligations simply slithered out of the ranks of the farming community and joined the swelling mass of landless labourers.

By the end of Elizabeth's reign, perhaps quarter of the population of Wales fell into the latter category, the great majority working on the land or in industries dependent upon

agriculture. The general conditions affecting their employment were set out in the *Statute of Artificers* (1563), a measure which consolidated much earlier legislation and which was, according to its preamble, intended to 'banish idleness, advance husbandry, and yield unto the hired person both in time of scarcity and in the
B.8 time of plenty a convenient proportion of wages' (B.8). Amongst other provisions the act stipulates that well-to-do farmers could force the children of the rural poor to serve as so-called 'apprentices in husbandry' from the age of ten until they were twenty-one, that unemployed men between the ages of twelve and sixty could be compelled to work as agricultural labourers, and that single women between the ages of twelve and forty could be committed to ward and forced to work. Wage rates for the lower orders were fixed annually by justices of the peace and tended to lag further and further behind the rate of inflation. The whole system ensured the existence of a large pool of cheap labour and subjected the labouring classes to tight social discipline.

Farm workers fell into two distinct categories. Unmarried farm servants lived with their employers and were hired by the year, frequently at autumnal 'hiring fairs' but also at 'hiring sessions' held under the supervision of local JPs and high constables. They received board and lodging, small cash wages,
B.9 and often their clothing (B.9). Maidservants usually slept in the farmhouse and menservants in the outbuildings, an arrangement which lasted until the early part of this century. They were often kept in order by strict discipline and physical chastizement, but if they worked satisfactorily they enjoyed a reasonable degree of security. Such was not the case with married farm labourers, who were employed, often irregularly, at such low rates of pay that all but the very youngest members of their family were
B.10 forced to work (B.10). They lived, for the most part, in squalid impermanent houses, had few material possessions, spent most of their lives out of doors, and were greatly dependent upon the goodwill of neighbouring farmers. When they proved insubordinate or unwilling to work they were liable to be despatched by the local JPs and high constables to the 'House of Correction' in the county town, where conditions were so harsh that they soon learned to be answerable to the demands of their betters.

Few documentary sources refer to the problem of poverty in Wales before the passing of the 1536 *Act of Union*, but from about that time public authorities became increasingly concerned about it, partly, no doubt, from compassion, but also out of concern lest widespread pauperism might lead to increased disorders and crime and out of a desire to keep poor rates as low as possible. The principal reason for the growth of pauperism in the sixteenth century was that the population was rising rapidly whereas the supply of peasant smallholdings was not, but bad harvests, trade depressions and purely local economic difficulties exacerbated the problem from time to time. Tudor governments had no means of tackling the basic causes of increased pauperism: instead they endeavoured to cope with its symptoms, and this they did in a series of statutes and royal proclamations culminating in the famous *Poor Law of 1598*. A policy evolved of dividing the poor into a number of broad categories, each of which received different treatment. The 'deserving poor', a group embracing orphans, abandoned children, cripples, aged people without any means of support and those able-bodied paupers who were willing to work but unable to find employment, were to be given relief either at home or in alms houses, whilst 'rogues and vagabonds' were to be harried and punished and, wherever possible, forced to settle down. In theory all the settled poor were to be under close control and supervision. Periodically they were rounded up and forced to attend 'sessions for labourers', where local JPs sought to enforce the provisions of the *Statute of Artificers*, notably by apprenticing older children, finding work for adults, and punishing the disobedient and
B.11 work-shy (B.11). They also appointed guardians of the poor within each parish who were authorized to raise poor rates, house, feed and clothe the homeless poor, and dole out supplementary relief wherever necessary. The task of bringing the vagrant poor to heel was entrusted to the unpaid parish constables who were instructed to arrest them, whip them soundly, and send them back to their birthplaces or last known
B.12 place of settlement (B.12). What is remarkable is that so many paupers continued to wander the countryside despite the harshness of the law and the rigour with which it was enforced. Undoubtedly, some vagrants were rogues who terrorized and

preyed upon ordinary householders, especially those living in remote places, but others were simply seeking to escape starvation or the persecution of officials, or else in search of work. Whatever the reason, the official view was that the poor were not supposed to wander far from their homes unless instructed to do so by their masters and in possession of a chit or letter of authorization. There were timorous, lazy and merciful constables who turned a blind eye to their activities, but they themselves were liable to punishment for neglect of duty. Late in Elizabeth's reign provost marshals and posses were employed in hunting down vagrants and meting out arbitrary punishment, but despite this draconian approach to the problem a writer of James I's reign could note that there were still thousands of vagrants in the country who had never known a settled home in their lives.

Many of the footloose poor made their way towards the towns of Wales and the borderland, and some went even further afield. During a purge of vagrant rogues in London in 1582 it was noted that many were Welsh but that few had been in the capital for more than three or four months, and when the city fathers of Worcester discussed the influx of poor people into their city two years later it was alleged that most had come from Wales. Within Wales itself towns were small, and it is unlikely that more than ten per cent of the population were town-dwellers (it has been estimated that in Elizabethan Glamorgan about one person in seven lived in a town, but the proportion was almost certainly lower in most other Welsh shires). Each town had a clearly defined social hierarchy. Most were run by small groups of wealthy *burgesses* who claimed gentry status and were frequently descended from *cadet* branches of local gentry families. Even poorer members of town councils often termed themselves 'gentlemen' by virtue of their office, though it is doubtful whether the county gentry would have accepted their pretensions. For the rest, urban status was largely a matter of wealth, and all towns rested solidly on a substantial stratum of unprivileged residents.

In town and countryside alike, the prime concern of most Tudor Welshmen was with the survival of their families, which hinged primarily upon the quality of the harvest. Milk and milk products, together with bread and other farinaceous foodstuffs, formed the basis of their diet. The bread of the poor varied considerably in composition from district to district, and when corn was in short supply it was often made partly of peas and beans. They ate little butchers' meat but exploited all local sources of food, including small birds, rabbits, hares, eels and fish: indeed, no fewer than 163 days in the year were 'fish-days' when the eating of flesh was proscribed. In times of extremity the poor fell back on a whole range of substitute foods, including roots, berries and bark, a situation which led inevitably to malnutrition, vulnerability to illness, epidemic diseases and dramatic increases in death rates. When ill or injured the lower orders had recourse, not to qualified physicians, but to the elders, 'white witches' and 'wizards', and sometimes the priests, of their local communities, and in times of dire distress to the apothecaries and barber-surgeons of nearby towns. Physical drudgery was part of everyday life.

The main source of energy available to the peasantry was muscle-power, and the working day lasted from dawn to dusk in winter and from 5am until after 7pm in summer. Until 1552 there were forty-three 'holy days' or holidays in the year, apart from Sundays, but a statute of that year reduced the number to twenty-three, though *George Owen* of Henllys observed in his common-place book that an extra holiday, the feast of St Curig on 16 June, was also observed. What sustained men under these circumstances was stoicism, good humour, the appreciation of pleasures now rare — the beauty of an undesecrated landscape, the richness of their orally-transmitted cultures, close family ties, the gaiety of
B.13 communal recreation (B.13) counted for much — and, as a counterpoise to the harshness of their everyday lives, a religious faith which offered the prospect of eternal joy to all who lived by the precepts and instructions of the priests, masters and local magnates who ruled their little worlds.

## Sources

B.1 And first I will begin with the tenants of the country, wherein I speak in general, including therein the greatest number, which in times past were tenants at will, and few sought leases, for most commonly the landlord rather made suit for a good tenant to take his land than the tenant to the landlord. Such was the scarcity of good tenants in those days there to be found that glad was the lord to hit upon a good, thrifty and husbandly tenant and, as for fines (sums of money payable to landlords at the beginning of tenancies) to be paid, it was not a thing known among them a hundred years past, saving only an earnest penny at the bargain-making . . . In these sixty years the poor tenants were wont to say that the paying of fines was an ill custom raised among them of late . . . But this ancient good custom within these forty years past is sore shaken and almost banished the country, for now the poor tenant that lived well in that golden world is taught to sing unto his lord a new song . . . And standeth so in bodily fear of his greedy neighbour that two or three years ere his lease ends he must bow to his lord for a new lease, and must pinch it out many years to heap money together . . .

(George Owen, *The Description of Penbrockshire,* 1603, ed. Henry Owen, 1, 1892, pp.190–1).

B.2 Almighty God hath created and appointed all things in heaven, earth and waters, in a most excellent and perfect order. In heaven He hath appointed distinct and several orders and states of Archangels and Angels. In earth he hath assigned and appointed Kings, Princes, with other Governors under them, in all good and necessary order . . . Every degree of people in their vocation, calling and office hath appointed to them their duty and order: some are in high degree, some in low, some Kings and Princes, some inferiors and subjects, priests and laymen, masters and servants, fathers and children, husbands and wives, rich and poor: and everyone hath need of other . . . Take away Kings, Princes, rulers, magistrates, judges and such estates God's order . . . and there must needs follow all mischief and utter destruction both of souls, bodies, goods, and commonwealths.

(The homily of Obedience, 1547).

B.3 The fourth sort or class amongst us is . . . day labourers, poor *husbandmen*, yea merchants or retailers which have no free land, *copyholders* and all artificers . . . These have no voice or authority in our commonwealth, and no account is made of them, but only to be ruled.

(Sir Thomas Smith, *The Commonwealth of England*, 1583).

B.4 *Household goods of a yeoman*

2 feather beds 40*s*; 2 caddows [rough woollen coverings] 40*s*; 2 pairs sheets 10*s*; 2 blankets 4*s*; 2 bolsters, 2 pillows 4*s*; 1 standing bedstead 10*s*; 1 cupboard 10*s*; 1 old 'bord' [table] 12*d*; 1 chair 12*d*; 1 trunk 10*s*; 1 old chest *4d*; 1 truckle bed 2*s*; 1 carpet for a round table 2*s*; 2 tablecloths for a round table and 1 for a long table 5*s*; 1 long table board with a frame 5*s*; 1 old skew [a high-backed wooden settle whose seat formed the lid of a coffer] 2*s*; 2 forms 12*d*; 6 brass pans, 1 cauldron 40*s*; 3 crocks of brass 12*s*; 3 hoopheads, 1 pipe, kive, 1 kinderkin 10*s*; 2 winnowing sheets, 2 sacks 4*s*; 26 pieces of pewter 12*s*; 4 brass candlesticks 4*s*; 1 pewter salt cellar 6*d*; 2 brandises [trivets] 12*d*; 1 brush, 1 frying pan 2*s*; 4 silver spoons 12*s*; 1 little bedstead 6*d*; 1 lantern, 4 stone troughs 4*s*; 1 iron grate 2*s*; 1 churn 12*d*; 1 bucket 3*d*; 1 cloak 40*s*; 1 pewter chamber pot 12 *d*.

*Total value of all his goods and chattels — £93*

(National Library of Wales: probate inventory of Peter Cheane of Walwyn's Castle, 1601).

B.5 It is necessary that by your precept to the constables of the hundreds, and other like officers, all able men from 16 years of age upwards within the limits of your commission in parish, hamlet or village, be sworn to appear at a day and place fixed for musters . . . Therefore it shall be well done to command that the names and surnames of all such persons able to bear arms be immediately written down by the constables of the hundreds or other officers, naming every householder by himself with his sons, menservants, apprentices, journeymen or other sojourners or indwellers able to bear arms, and that the said householder be

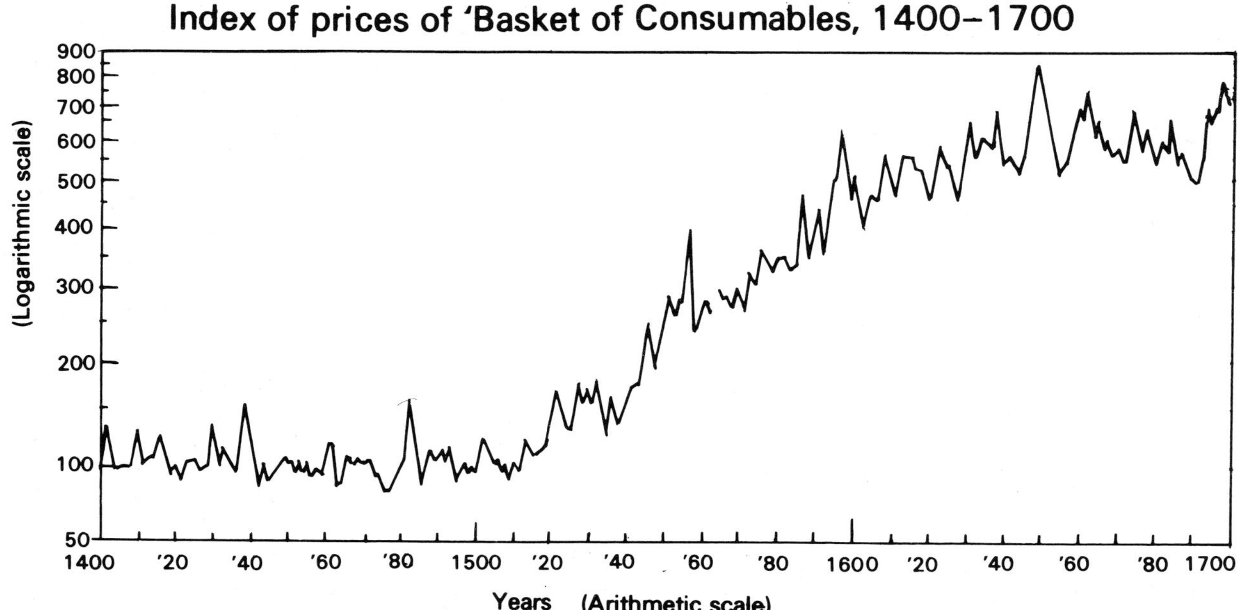


Index of Prices of Basket of Consumables 1400–1700.

This graph demonstrates the dramatic inflation in prices in the Tudor period. Prices remain relatively stable between 1400 and 1500, hovering around the notional index figure of 100. Then, from 1500–1600, the increase in prices is dramatic, indicating a six-fold increase (600 on the index) around 1600. The rate of increase then levels off.

charged to bring all the said persons with their armour or weapons at such times as shall be limited.

(Privy Council to the commissioner appointed for taking general musters in Denbighshire, 1580, in R. Flenley (ed.), *A calendar of the register of the Council in the Marches of Wales*, pp.200–1).

B.6 *Household goods of a husbandman*

1 cauldron 10*s*; 3 pans 10*s*; 1 crock, 1 posnet [small pan with a handle and three feet] 4*s*; frying pan 6*d*; 5 pewter dishes 3*s* 4*d*; 1 pewter pot 6*d*; 2 candlesticks 12*d*; 1 cupboard 2*s*; 1 skew 3*s* 4*d*; 1 'turn' [spinning wheel] 6*d*; 1 pair of hand cards 4*d*; a table board with frame 6*s* 8*d*; 1 form 6*d*; 2 coffers 2*s*; 1 brush 12*d*; 1 brandiron 6*d*; 2 bedsteads 2*s*; 2 pairs blankets, 1 coverlet 6*s*; 1 bolster 12*d*; a coal chimney 5*s*; 2 'brassattes' [brass vessels?] 12*d*; 1 stand 12*d*; 1 bucket 3*d*; 1 hutch 12*d*.

*Total value of all his goods and chattels* — *£16..14*s..*4*d.

(National Library of Wales: probate inventory of Lewis Gibbon of Uzmaston, 1601).

B.7 First, as touching the trade of life, the poorest *husbandman* liveth upon his own travail [labour], having corn, butter, cheese, beef, mutton, poultry and the like of his own sufficient to maintain his house. He maketh the apparel of him and his family of his own wool and seldom useth any money, but those that want such necessaries are driven to buy altogether in a manner at days [i.e on credit, days being fixed for repayment], for seldom buyeth any of the poorer sort anything for ready money. Corn, butter, cheese, wool and such like the poor man buyeth of his rich neighbour at days and commonly their payments are from May to mid-November, for all that while is the country of Wales full of fairs. Then are their cattle, sheep, lambs, swine, wool and other matters in price so that he that hath any of these to sell all the summer shall be sure of money. But from November to May they have nothing wherewith to make money . . . so that whatsoever you sell they will have a day of payment till summer or else they will not deal with you. Likewise for their iron, salt, oil, lincloth, pitch, tar, spice and such things that are to be had out of towns, the townsman selleth the same at days also, and of all these things that he buyeth he seldom or never buyeth the value of 40*s*. of any one man . . . And thus much for the order and trade of living used by the poorer sort of people in Wales, whereby this multitude of small actions ariseth, for there are none but the poorer sort of people that are sued in these base courts.

(George Owen, *The Dialogue of the Government of Wales*, 1594, ed. Henry Owen, I, 1982).

B.8 Every person between the age of 12 years and the age of 60 years not being lawfully retained nor apprentice [apart from a number of listed exemptions] . . . nor having a father or mother then living or other ancestor whose heir apparent he is having lands [etc.] of the yearly value of £10 or above, or goods or chattels of the value of £40, nor being a necessary or convenient officer or servant lawfully retained as is aforesaid, nor having a convenient farm or holding . . . shall . . . by virtue of this statute be compelled to be retained to serve in husbandry by the year with any person that keepeth husbandry and will require any such person so to serve . . .

Two justices of peace, the mayor or other head officer of any city [etc.] and two aldermen or two other discreet *burgesses* . . . if there be no aldermen, may appoint any such woman as is of the age of 12 years and under the age of 40 years and unmarried and forth of service . . . to be retained or serve by the year or by the week or day for such wages and in such reasonable sort as they shall think meet . . .

And for the better advancement of husbandry and tillage and to the intent that such as are fit to be made apprentices to husbandry may be bounden thereunto . . . every person being a householder and having half a ploughland at the least in tillage may receive as an apprentice any person above the age of 10 years and under the age of 18 years to serve in husbandry until his age of 21 years at the least, or until the age of 24 years as the parties can agree . . .

(Statute of Artificers, 1563. A.E. Bland, P.A. Brown and R.H. Tawney (eds.), *English Economic History. Select Documents*, pp.326–30).

B.9 *The overall annual profit of a farm*

Courthall [Cwrt, Eglwyswrw, was a farm belonging to *George Owen* of Henllys]. 12 November 1593 . . .

People in household and daily charge in the farm and labour aforesaid.

| | | |
|---|---|---|
| | The ploughman or chief servant | |
| | His wife | |
| *persons* | One other man servant | |
| *in* | | 8 persons . . . |
| *house* | Two ploughboys | |
| | One shepherd | |
| | Two labouring maids | |

26 bushels of corn yearly allowed towards the maintaining of the said 8 persons in the year i.e. half a bushel weekly at 6*s*.8*d*. the bushel — £9 6*s*.8*d*.

4 bushels of oaten malt allowed for their drink from Allhallowtide till May, during which time there is no store of milk to be had, 5*s*. the bushel — 20*s* . . .

Item, allowed them 13*s*.4*d*. for providing of flesh against certain feasts in the year — 13*s*.4*d*.

6 stones of cheese and 6 gallons of butter allowed them from November till May for their finding during that space, during which time there is no milk to be had. Valued at 5s. the stone and the gallon — £3.

In candles allowed them in the winter time — 2*s* . . .

Wages to the man and his wife for the year — 46*s*.8*d*.

To the second ploughman for the year — 16*s*.8*d*.

To two ploughboys 8*s*.4*d*. apiece — 16*s*.8*d*.

To the shepherd — 13*s*.4*d*.

To two labouring maids 12*s* apiece — 24*s* . . .

Bedclothes yearly about my said people which will be worn, in average years worth — 10*s* . . .

Offerings in the Church for the said 8 persons at 3 1/2*d*. apiece in the year — 12*d*.[*sic*] . . .

The hire of 240 persons in harvest besides my own servants, reaping and binding, men at 3*d*. and women at 2*d*. the day — 47*s*.4*d*. [He is referring not to the employment of 240 people, but to payments for 240 working days].

(George Owen, *The Taylors Cussion*, Part 1, ff.33–4).

B.10 What I shall speak here touching the constitution of the bodies of the people of this country must be understood of the general and common sort of people in the country, being the greatest number, and not of the gentlemen, serving-men or townsmen . . . This kind of people I find to be very mean [poor] and simple, short of growth, broad and shrubby [under-sized] . . . The cause of this disability of persons is easily to be discerned if a man looks into the state of the country and education of the meaner sort of people . . . for I have by good account numbered three thousand young people to be brought up continually in herding of cattle within this shire [Pembrokeshire], who are put to this idle education when they are first come to be ten or twelve years of age and turned to the open fields to follow their cattle, when they are forced to endure the heat of the sun in his greatest extremity to parch and burn their faces, hands, legs, feet and breasts in such sort as they seem more like tawny Moors than people of this land. And then with the cold, frost, snow, hail and wind they are so tormented, having the skin of their legs, hands, face and feet all in chinks and chaps . . . that, poor fools, they may well hold opinion with the papists that there is a purgatory . . .

And when they have redeemed their liberty out of this purgatory by attaining to twenty or twenty four years of age, then are they held in such continual labour in tilling of the land, burning of lime, digging of coals, and other slaveries and extreme toils, as while they live they never come in shape, favour or comeliness to be accounted among the number of personable men, and yet perchance, his deformity notwithstanding, as serviceable in proof as he that looketh with a fairer countenance . . . The gentlemen, serving men and the townsmen of this country are not so unserviceable, but are very personable, comely and tall men, which confirmeth my former assertion that the hard labour, parching of the sun and starving [suffering greatly] with cold is a chief cause of the unseemliness of the common people of this country, seeing the gentlemen, serving men and those brought up in towns, which are not tormented with these extremities of heat and cold, nor tired with toil, do prove more personable. And of the common people of this country the Welshmen, whom the rest call 'the mountain men', are found to

Reaping scene from Holinshed's *Chronicles*, 1577. (*Source: BBC Hulton Picture Library.*)

be the more personable, as men not so cloyed with labour as those that live by tillage.

(George Owen, *The Description of Penbrockshire, 1603*, ed. Henry Owen, 1, 1892, pp.41–4).

B.11 [He is to summon a jury of 24 substantial freeholders and all the high and petty constables of Cemais and Cilgerran hundreds to appear before the local JPs at Newport, the latter] . . . having with them fair written the names and surnames of all day labourers, artificers and masterless servants being above the age of twelve years and under the age of threescore, and all cottagers such as have not sufficient land belonging to their houses, farms and tenements to employ their labour about tilling and working thereof . . . and all other[s] that are compellable to serve by the laws and statutes of this realm, and that you do give in charge that the said petty constables do warn . . . every of them to be likewise there . . . and that you cause the said high constables and petty constables to arrest and attach all persons brought up in any of the arts or sciences specified in the said statute made in the fifth year of the Queen's Majesty's reign [i.e. the *Statute of Artificers*, 1563], or that hath used any of the same arts for three years, and being under the age of 30 years or unmarried, and which refuse to serve in any of the said arts, and every other person from the age of 12 years to 60 that refuse to be retained by the year in husbandry; and also that they do attach all such persons that depart from one town, hundred or shire to another without a testimonial of his departure thence, and all persons that retain any such person into service so departing without licence, and all persons retained in building or other work and that departeth before the work finished; and also all artificers, craftsmen, labourers and other persons that giveth or receiveth excessive wages or hire . . . and also . . . all persons between the age of ten years and eighteen years which are compellable at yet refuse to be bound 'prentice in husbandry . . .

(Form of a warrant to the sheriff for summoning a sessions for labourers, in George Owen, *The Taylors Cussion*, Part 1, ff.87–87d.).

B.12 On the 20th August, strict watch is to be kept, as well throughout the shires as in places exempt, from 7 p.m. to 3 o'clock next afternoon by constables and two, three or more of the most substantial parishioners. All rogues, vagabonds and masterless men are to be arrested and punished by stocking and sharp and severe whipping according to the laws, afterwards sending them on, from constable to constable, until they reach their native place or last abode within three years . . . Similarly action shall be taken on the 12th September and October and then each 15 or 20 days, not omitting to punish any vagabond found between the specified times . . . Hampton Court, 30th July 1571.

(Letter from the Privy Council to the Council in the Marches of Wales, in R. Flenley (ed.), *A calendar of the register of the Council in the Marches of Wales*, p.96).

B.13 *North Wales, circa 1600*

Upon the Sundays and holiday (holy days) the multitude of all sorts of men, women and children of every parish to use to meet in sundry places, either on some hill or on the side of some mountain, where their harpers and crowthers (fiddlers) sing them songs of the doings of their ancestors, namely of their wars against the kings of this realm and the English nation. And then do they rip up their pedigrees at length, how each of them is descended from those their old princes.

(British Library, Lansdowne MS 111, f.10).

## Debating the Evidence

The documents which Brian Howells uses are similar in many respects to those used by Gwynfor Jones in his material on the gentry. They are mainly commentaries by contemporary writers, lists of possessions and estate records. Again, that doyen of Welsh Elizabethan historians, *George Owen* of Henllys, is an invaluable source of information. There is one crucial difference. In the previous section, gentlemen antiquaries were analysing and commenting on their own class. In this section they are observing their inferiors, socially and in terms of wealth and lifestyle. The controllers or arbiters of Tudor society in the local community across Wales were the gentry. Their evidence about the lower orders is invaluable but is bound to present us with a much less complete picture, and a less reliable picture, than when the gentry comment on their own attitudes. There are whole areas of the experience of the lower orders which are likely to remain closed to us because as a group they left no record.

*Source B.1*
Given that *George Owen* himself was the owner of a sizeable estate what evidence is there here to suggest that his comments on the fate of tenants are likely to be true? Why might he take such a sympathetic view towards *leaseholders*?

*Source B.2*
In what kind of society do you think a document such as this would be necessary? From what directions, if any, might a challenge to this hierarchic view of social relationships be mounted?

*Source B.3*
Should historians be wary of contemporary social categorization? Do you think Sir Thomas Smith means the same by 'class' as we would today? What do Documents B.2 and B.3 have in common? What do they tell us about Tudor society?

*Source B.4*
Compare this document with A.7. Purely on the basis of these documents, would you say it was easy to categorize Tudor gentry and Tudor *yeomen*?

*Source B.5*
What view of social responsibility (especially of the role of the householder) is presented by this order?

*Source B.6*
In what ways would you regard this as a reliable source for assessing the manner in which a Tudor *husbandman* lived?

*Source B.7*
What do *George Owen*'s observations tell us about economic activity in Tudor Wales? According to this document what were the major items

and channels of exchange in a rural society? This appears to be an objective account of the lifestyle of a Tudor *husbandman*. *George Owen* was a gentleman. Where would he have got his information about 'the poorer sort of people'?

*Source B.8*
The source is about the control of young labourers, but what does it tell us about Elizabethan government? And what does it tell us about contemporary perceptions of minimum income, labour mobility, attitude to work and the relationship between vagrancy and disorder?

*Source B.9*
What can this kind of document tell us about the diet and living standards of farm labourers and of the hierarchy of status within their ranks?

*Source B.10*
How do you explain the keen social observation and wide social sympathies of *George Owen* as revealed by this passage? There are many artistic representations of gentry and some of 'the common sort of people' — for example, the paintings of Brueghel. If you can find some of these see if the evidence of the paintings supports the evidence of B.10.

*Source B.11*
What specialist terms in this document need explanation before the historian could make full use of it? How far did Tudor governance in the localities, as revealed by this document, rely on local juries and the compilation of written evidence?

*Source B.12*
What does this source tell us about the attitude of government to the poor of Tudor Wales? There was an increase in population and dramatic inflation during the sixteenth century. What effect do you think this might have on the incidence of poverty?

*Source B.13*
The authorship of this document is not given here. How would this reflect on the use to which you put it? What is the only *certain* statement

you could make on the basis of this one document? How far does this document reveal the degree to which traditional customs and hatreds survived in Wales in spite of the 'joyful metamorphosis' referred to in Document A.17?

**Discussion**

It is very difficult to rescue the mass of people in Tudor Wales from the relative oblivion to which, for so long, historians consigned them. The mass of the population wrote nothing down for the simple reason that they could not write, nor could they read. We must here exercise the essential historical skill of empathy. Our immediate reaction is that this illiteracy must have been a terrible handicap to them and certainly a source of cultural impoverishment. In fact, in the Tudor period, it was neither. Medieval culture, for all but the very few, was an oral and visual culture. Education was largely for clerics and, through them, the administration of government and justice. Two things fundamentally altered this situation. First there was the invention of the printing press; second, the Reformation. The printing press produced a revolution in communications, and the potential for change which a literate population implies, a change as great as any in human history. The Reformation required, in time, a literate population so that people could read the Bible and save their souls. The replacement of the Roman Catholic church as the State church also implied the lingering death of major elements in medieval culture — the mystery and miracle plays, the saints days, the iconography of paintings and statues in churches, the pilgrimages. The Tudor period in England and in Wales saw the beginnings of a revolution in education, culture and religion. However, these changes affected the upper ranks of society to an immeasurably greater extent than the lower. According to Rosemary O'Day, *Education and Society 1500–1800*, (1982, pp.17–21), it seems likely that even by the *seventeenth* century literacy rates for the population of England were no more than 30 per cent and in England we are dealing with a population whose language was that of the increasing numbers of printed books. In Wales, only the gentry and a proportion of *yeomen*, of the lay population, spoke English and were literate, probably under 5 per cent of the population. The accounts we have of the social orders, therefore, are those of people of the status of the Englishman Sir Thomas Smith (B.3), and Welsh gentry such as *George Owen* (B.7), whose evidence on almost all aspects of life in Elizabethan Wales is so vital.

The view which is presented of vagrants, of landless labourers, and of poor tenants in these documents is, therefore, a view from above (B.1, B.10). The statutes quoted here are reliable evidence of some of the measures by which parliament controlled the labour of the poorer orders. Sir Thomas Smith is certainly to be trusted if what we are looking for is an insight into the attitude towards the governed by the governors (B.3). The Homily of Obedience (B.2) provides adequate supporting evidence for Smith's view. The inventories (B.4, B.6) which furnish lists of the possessions of a *yeoman* or a *husbandman* provide an invaluable glimpse into both the scale of their wealth and their lifestyle. We would still need to know whether these were representative lists, and why they were drawn up. If, for example, any kind of taxation depended on the scale of possessions it is likely that the family of a *yeoman* or *husbandman* would seek to minimize their number.

Perhaps the abiding impression, once more, is the richness of *George Owen*'s evidence (B.1, B.7, B.9, B.10, B.11). He was one of a new breed in Tudor times, the learned local historian or antiquary who recorded in meticulous detail impressions of what he saw around him (see below, p.105). This was a different kind of history from that which was practised by the *bards* who recounted the glories and gifts of their patrons and the achievements of their patrons' ancestors. It makes possible the writing of a different scale of history by modern historians. Much of the evidence *seems* to be impressive in its neutrality. Document B.1 is an excellent example here. *George Owen* is drawing attention to the plight of tenants in Elizabethan times compared with their former situation when there was less land hunger, more farms for rent, and therefore a different relationship between landlord and tenant. Since *George Owen* was himself a landlord leasing farms to tenants, it seems likely that his generally sympathetic attitude to the plight of tenants accurately reflects the current situation. At the same time it highlights the deficiencies of the evidence relating to the lower classes. They do not speak for themselves.

# *Country and Town: Agrarian Change and Urban Fortunes*

MATTHEW GRIFFITHS

They have begun of late to lime their land
And plough the ground where sturdy oaks did stand, . . .

Churchyard's eulogy of agricultural improvement in late six-
C.1 teenth-century Wales (C.1) may be poor stuff as poetry, but it undeniably conveys something of the spirit of a great movement underway to extend the margins of human colonization and turn moorland and marsh into productive land. This movement was part of a larger process whose end result was a widespread transformation of landscape and society under the pressures of population growth and expanding demand. During the same period Welsh towns, their fortunes intimately bound up with developments in the countryside, experienced more chequered fortunes. By the later years of Queen Elizabeth's reign, however, there are signs of a revival in urban life and trade.

Economic and social trends of the kind that will be discussed here do not fit neatly into the reigns of kings and queens, nor can they be confined within the lifespan of a dynasty. It is under the Tudors, nonetheless, that we can discern processes that have their origins in the fourteenth century and which continue in the seventeenth century restructuring the physical appearance of the countryside and the social structure that inhabited it onto lines that are familiar to us today. Especially after about 1550 population growth seems to give added impetus to changes that began under a very different demographic regime.

An understanding of the history of Welsh population is the key to understanding the economic changes that take place in Tudor Wales. This is not to claim that population movements are autonomous factors; the rise and fall of population is itself generated by changes in the organization and relations of production. For our purpose here, however, we need simply to remember that the Black Death and subsequent epidemics reduced the population of Wales by a third to a half after 1350. There are strong signs, however, that plague attacked a population which may already have been shrinking due to difficulties in producing sufficient food to supply a society that was the culmination of two centuries of demographic growth and expanding settlement. In the decade after 1400 the rebellion of *Owain Glyndŵr* brought distress and further depopulation. Together, plague and war accelerated the pace of developments visible in early fourteenth-century Wales: the commutation of services and renders; the decline of *serfdom* and *bond tenancy*; the disintegration of *clanlands* and *bond hamlets*; the leasing of *seigneurial demesnes*.

In the fifteenth century, with population at a lower level, land and food relatively cheap and labour much scarcer, the early modern Welsh economy began to take shape. In particular, the century after 1450 witnesses the growth of the cattle and cloth trades as the mainstays of agriculture over much of Wales. At the same time a reorganization of farms and settlement was underway in native Wales and in the manorialized *Englishries* of the coastal and border lowlands alike. By the early sixteenth century the population of Wales appears to have been rising once more — a result, in part at least, of better diet and living conditions. By 1550, the population stood at about 225,000; by the reign of Charles II (we lack any intermediate data) it had climbed by 50 per cent again, to around 372,000. If the Welsh experience paralleled that traced in detail for England, then population growth was steepest between 1540 and 1600, less dramatic thereafter, with little or no increase between 1650 and the early eighteenth century. Population growth was sustained in England and Wales despite the fact that epidemic disease and harvest failure could bring periods of severe distress and high mortality — in the late 1550s,
C.2 for example, or the mid 1590s (C.2). In the middle of the sixteenth
C.3 century (C.3) it was the most productive southern counties of Wales that were most densely peopled. The predominantly upland shires of central and north Wales (and likewise the hilly interiors of Glamorgan and western Monmouthshire) were much more

thinly inhabited. This pattern was maintained until the Industrial Revolution. However, it is noteworthy that between the reign of Mary and the *Restoration*, population growth in Wales was most marked in the uplands, and especially this was so in north Wales. On one writer's calculation, (Frank Emery in Joan Thirsk, ed., *The Agrarian History of England and Wales, 1540–1640*, Cambridge, 1967, pp.393–428) the population of Merioneth increased in this period by about 85 per cent, that of Caernarfon by 76 per cent, and that of Anglesey by 66 per cent. These figures bear witness to the more intensive use of land and the colonization from the waste that took place in the sixteenth century as responses to increasing population.

This reshaping of the pattern of rural life had started, however, long before population began to rise. In native Wales — where Welsh law and custom rather than English practices prevailed — this reshaping was already well developed by the middle of the fifteenth century. The Welsh practice of *cyfran* — *gavelkind* to English lawyers — whereby a man's landholding would be divided on his death equally amongst his heirs, had reduced the tenements of many freemen to a size which was no longer capable of feeding a family. At the same time, many communities of bond tenants had become depopulated through plague and war. These processes brought land on the market, and there were many in the Wales of the fifteenth century — native *uchelwyr*, settler *burgesses* from the towns, the officialdom of the Principalities of North and South Wales — with the resources to purchase such land. Activity in the land market fuelled the growth of a new and confident gentry eager by the 1530s for political status commensurate with their economic influence; the purchase of land and the accumulation of estates also brought about changes in the physical appearance of the countryside. In much of north and west Wales medieval settlement was quite strongly *nucleated*, though the farmsteads of the *clanlands* were more loosely associated than the cottages of bondmen. Settlement was linked too with the cultivation of small arable open fields or *sharelands* in which the strips of individual farmers were intermingled. Beyond these *sharelands* lay common meadow and pasture land. The purchase of fragmented holdings in the *clanlands* encouraged the amalgamation of open field strips and the enclosure with wall or hedge of the larger fields that were created. Enclosure was also the fate of the land belonging to the *empty bond vills*, whether it was acquired legally by estate builders or by the *encroachment* of neighbours. *Nucleated* settlement was gradually being replaced by a countryside of isolated farms surrounded by enclosed fields of the kind we expect to see today. There is some doubt as to how far parts of upland south Wales — Glamorgan or Gwent for example — shared the agrarian pattern of native society in Caernarfon or Cardigan, but what research has been done strongly suggests a similar and contemporary amalgamation of *morcellated* freeholdings, the creation of larger farmsteads through purchase, and the emergence of a new *rentier* gentry class.

In the manors of the borders and the coastal lowlands of southern Glamorgan, Gwent and Pembroke analogous developments were underway in the fifteenth century, though these have been explored less thoroughly. In many parishes the open fields were in retreat by the reign of Henry VIII. Declining population had meant that in these communities, too, there was land available in the later Middle Ages. The high price of labour had forced manorial lords to withdraw from the direct exploitation of their *demesnes*, and these became available for leasing in parcels or *en bloc*. Abandoned *villein holdings* were also liable to engrossment. There was therefore a tendency towards larger farms. In some Vale of Glamorgan communities it is possible to see clearly how small twelve- or fifteen-acre *villein holdings* — typical of the early fourteenth century — were replaced by the reign of Henry VIII by tenements of twenty to fifty acres. The engrossment of holdings and the leasing of demesne land was the opportunity to rationalize and intensify land use by the amalgamation of strips in the open fields and the planting of hedges to create enclosed fields. Where this process was taken to its logical conclusion (as in Barry, Glamorgan, by the later sixteenth century) fields were not only enclosed but a wholesale reorganization of farm layouts achieved so that farmers were freed from the need to cross other men's land to get to their own fields. Depopulation, involving the frequent physical shrinkage of villages and hamlets (sometimes their total desertion, though this occurred less often in south Wales than in England), thus created the opportunity to rationalize landholding and redistribute land in a buyer's market. In the Glamorgan of the

later sixteenth century *Rice Merrick* believed that the major enclos-
C.4 ures around his St Nicholas home had taken place before 1500 (C.4
C.5 and C.5).

By the time of *Bosworth Field* (1485) the pattern of future change within rural society had been set. The detailed working out of these processes, whether in the uplands or the lowlands, in native or in anglicized Wales has as yet been only tentatively traced although the end results are tangibly with us. We need much more local research to establish the precise chronology of change. Renewed population growth, however, seems to have given an added dimension to the remodelling of the landscape and the restructuring of society. In *Wallia pura*, the abolition of *cyfran* in the Union legislation made it much easier for men to hold on to land they had painstakingly acquired through manipulation of the complicated mortgaging procedures of Welsh customary law. Although it would be a long time before *partible inheritance* was totally abandoned, its disappearance in law gave a permanency to estates and an encouragement to estate builders. A concurrent development was the release of vast tracts of monastic land on to the market at the *dissolution of the monasteries*, further enabling the nascent gentry of Tudor Wales to extend and consolidate their property and social position. Above all, population growth, the consequent increase in demand for land on which to live, to pasture one's animals and grow crops, and the development of distance trade in cattle, accelerated the alienation and concentration of former *clanland*, the amalgamation of shareland, and the dispersal of rural settlement. A concomitant of this activity, in those townships which have been studied in detail, was the thoroughgoing consolidation and concentration of landholding into fewer hands, in the case of both tenanted farms and freeholds. By the reign of James I, farms of thirty to a hundred acres often stood where, a century previously, smallholdings of under a dozen acres had been typical. With the anciently settled land in fewer hands, an increasingly polarized society evolved containing rising numbers of landless labourers and migrants.

More dramatic than the slow disappearance of the *clanlands* and the consolidation of tenements, perhaps, is the process highlighted in Churchyard's *The Worthines of Wales* — the extension of the boundaries of human settlement and the colonization and enclosure of former common and waste land. Linked with this was the erosion of the ancient practice of *transhumance grazing*, the movement of cattle in late spring from lowland pastures to spend the summer months in the uplands. Especially after 1550, wasteland and common, whether the high *ffriddoedd* or ill-drained lowland marsh, became prey to *encroachment*, appropriation and enclosure by all classes in society. The stimulus was land hunger, whether that of the displaced poor looking for a few acres to settle, or that of the cormorant rich eager to maximize profits from the cattle trade.

The petition of the freeholders of Montgomery and Radnor
C.6 (C.6) illustrates this activity. When the *Council of the Marches* investigated its charges it recommended action against *encroachment* in Breconshire and Merioneth also. In the latter county a late sixteenth-century Crown rental lists over 400 *encroachments* — amounting to over 10,000 acres in four *commotes*. Legal action commenced by the Earl of Worcester in the 1590s against freeholders and tenants in his lordship of Gower documents the same tendencies and indicates that they were by no means confined to the upland margins. Seaside marsh was as vulnerable as moorland *ffridd* and the colonizers, as in mid Wales, represented all social classes, from the local gentry down to the poor seeking to
C.7 erect cottages along the common edge (C.7).

Colonization, *encroachment* and enclosure, the rationalization of landholding seem universal in the later sixteenth century. New lines of hedge or drystone wall marked out land claimed from the waste. As part of this process many *hafotai*, the summer shelters of *transhumance graziers*, became permanent dwellings; others were abandoned, their sites preserved in mounds of rubble and earth or in field names. In the anglicized lowlands, the enclosure of the open fields continued and in many parishes these had virtually disappeared by 1600. In others, however, remnants of the medieval field pattern survived into the eighteenth and occasionally the nineteenth centuries. The pace of enclosure was uneven. Why this was so is imperfectly understood. George Owen of Henllys gives an impression of rapid enclosure associated with the purchase and exchange of land in Pembrokeshire in the 1590s
C.8 (C.8), but truncated open fields persisted in parts of the county for many years to come. In Gower, likewise, the process was far from

general, and the survival of open field more marked than in the Vale of Glamorgan. In the latter area, too, open field disappeared more rapidly from some communities than others; developments in neighbouring parishes could be quite different. Factors that retarded enclosure may have included fragmented landownership, which would have inhibited the exchange of parcels needed to lay strips together and rationalize the layout of farmsteads, and variations in farm size. Gower tenants seem to have managed smaller farms than their Vale of Glamorgan equivalents and may have lacked the capital to carry out improvements. Farmers in Gower seem to have been unable to participate in the 'Great Rebuilding' of farmhouses underway in the southern Vale by the 1580s; again this may have been a function of lower profits.

The local history of the lowland landscape still remains to be written, but it seems clear that enclosure of the arable was not, as it so often was in sixteenth-century England, a contentious and socially divisive process. Nor was it accompanied by a recognizable shift away from tillage; the aim seems to have been an intensification of both corn growing and animal husbandry. Agriculture in lowland Gwent, Glamorgan and Pembroke was a mixed agriculture, though contemporaries tended to stress the quality of corn ground in these areas. Farmers were able therefore to take advantage of the profits to be made from sales of wheat and barley as prices climbed in the sixteenth century; equally they were well placed to meet the demands of Ireland and the west country for butter, wool, cloths, hides and livestock. At the same time as pastoralists in north and mid Wales became drawn into an economy centred on the cattle and cloth markets of the *Marches*, so the mixed farmers of the southern coast became integrated into a wider regional framework centred on Bristol.

The main lines of change in the Welsh countryside are clear, even if the exact timing of developments at the local level is uncertain. We can identify both the physical changes men made to their environment and the changes in social structure and tenures that accompanied them. Town and country in early modern society were intimately linked. Whatever its wider connections, the main reason for the existence of the town was to act as a centre for the exchange and distribution of the produce of its hinterland, and to provide the basic industrial commodities and specialized

services that rural communities required. However, the impact of fluctuations in the agrarian economy on the towns is poorly understood; at best it seems fair to suggest that expanding agriculture had a delayed effect on town life. Although population had begun to recover by the early sixteenth century from its late medieval slump, and although this recovery was reflected in both price increases for foodstuffs and animal produce at an early stage, it is not until the end of the Tudor period that unmistakable signs of urban growth appear. Medieval Wales had been endowed with far more boroughs and market centres than its economy could justify. Towns had developed, in the first place, to support the garrisons of castles on a hostile frontier and to attract colonizers in the wake of the small bands of soldiery who had wrested territory from native Welsh rulers. By the later Middle Ages most towns had lost their military and administrative roles. To survive as urban communities they required to be well sited in relation to communications and to be able to reap the benefits of trade with the countryside around them. Many towns lacked these attributes. Caerphilly in Glamorgan, for example, located on the edge of the uplands of Senghennydd, was too close to Cardiff and Newport to maintain a flourishing market. Dryslwyn and Dinefwr were too close to each other, and close, too, to Carmarthen, the capital of the southern Principality. Economic rationality, combined with the impact of plague and rebellion, meant that the fourteenth and fifteenth centuries saw a dwindling life in a goodly number of plantation boroughs. In some cases this decline was terminal and, as at Dryslwyn, the site of the borough became deserted. Other towns lost all urban pretensions as their markets failed and collapsed into the
C.9 condition of agricultural villages (C.9). The true victims of this
winnowing are easy to identify; it is more difficult to assess the fortunes of communities which retained a genuine town life.

By 'town life' we mean not just the possession of an active market, but the distinctive community associated with such a market. Mid-Tudor tax records enable us to demonstrate the concentration of wealth in towns such as Caernarfon or
C.10 Conway (C.10); they reveal, too, that the distribution of
wealth within towns was unlike that in a rural parish. Urban social structure, in the towns of Wales, as in their English

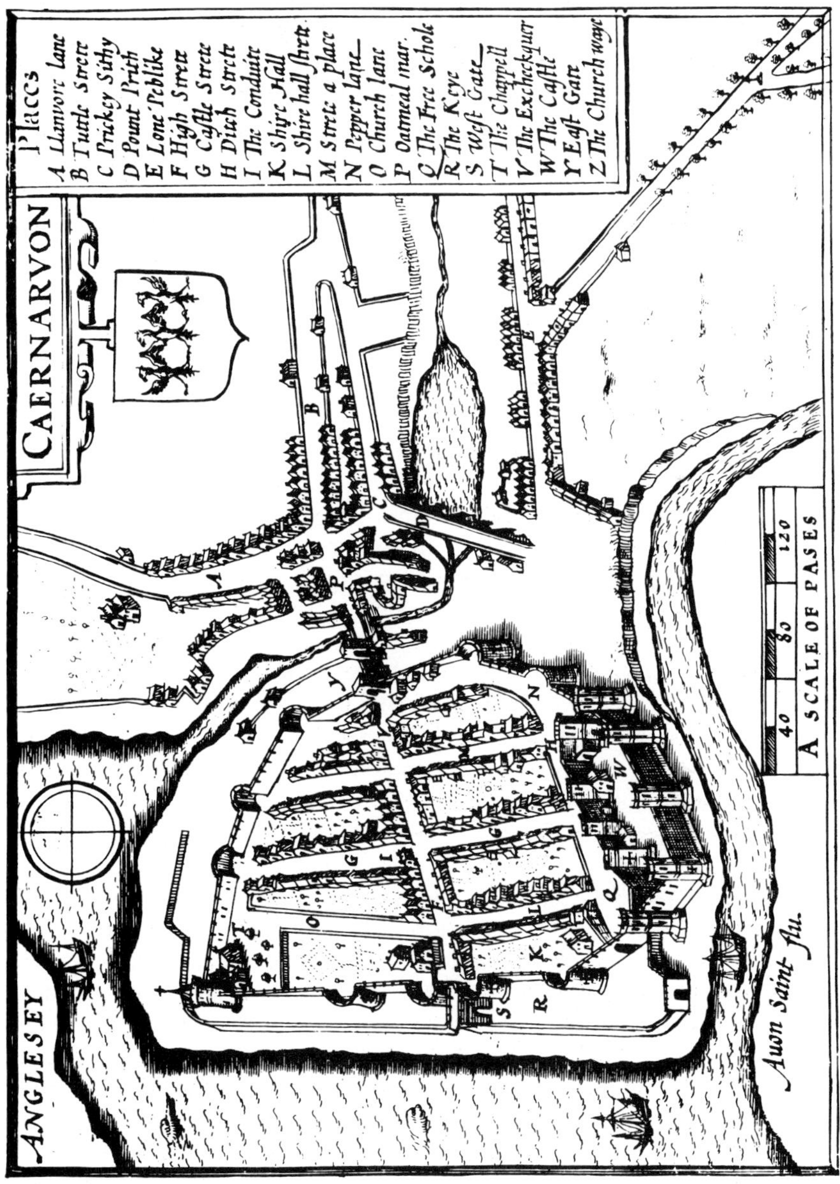


John Speed's map of Caernarfon, 1611. (*Source: National Library of Wales.*)

counterparts, was characterized by a broad base of folk living near or below the poverty line, generally engaged in casual and menial roles; a substantial middle class of smaller merchants, professionals, tradesmen and craftsmen; and a narrow elite of wealthy merchants and gentlemen. The larger towns in sixteenth-century Wales, Swansea or Haverfordwest, for example, were governed by increasingly exclusive civic oligarchies of rich *burgesses* and gentry. The occupational structure of towns was also unlike that of the countryside; even a small borough such as Cowbridge (Glamorgan) contained a greater diversity of occupations than a large village such as
C.11 nearby Llantwit Major. The reports of *Leland* and *Camden* (C.11,
C.12 C.12) suggest that the major boroughs at least had an appearance totally unlike that of the large village. Walls, though often in decay, proclaimed the separateness of an important borough; within the walls a regular pattern of *burgage plots* announced that these were often planned communities. Towns such as Pembroke and Cardiff, or the Edwardian boroughs of north Wales, were variations on the *bastides* of twelfth- and thirteenth-century England and *Gascony*. There was little change in the layout of most Welsh towns until industrialization; additional population in the sixteenth and seventeenth centuries was accommodated either by the subdivision of tenements or by *infilling*. The town plans of *Speed* confirm the accounts of *Camden* and *Leland*; there was generally plenty of room left within the walls, and in
C.11 addition the possibility of suburban expansion outside the walled
C.12 area (C.11, C.12, C.13).

C.13 Vacant space within the sixteenth-century town seems often to have been the result of shrinking population in the later Middle Ages. Declining population permanently reduced the status of some centres. In 1300 Tenby and Holt were amongst the largest boroughs, each with populations of about 1,500, while Chepstow, Usk, Cowbridge and Newport (Gwent) probably
C.14 numbered over 1,000 inhabitants. By 1550 (C.14) there had been a significant shift in urban ranking. Holt plummeted to no more than about 300 people and declined from a major borough to a local market centre with only pretensions to urbanity. There are exceptions. Carmarthen, a modest town of some 800 inhabitants in the thirteenth century, was by the middle of the sixteenth

century the largest town in Wales. In general, though, most towns experienced a contraction in numbers after 1350 and were smaller in 1550 than they had been 200 years previously. It is not surprising, then, that late medieval ministers' accounts and borough rentals contain lists of decayed *burgage plots*. In 1473/4, there were 127 such vacant tenements in Haverfordwest.

The significance of these observations in economic terms is, however, difficult to measure. Urban populations fell — but so did population generally. It is difficult to judge if major towns such as Cardiff, as well as losing people, also experienced an absolute contraction of their economies. There is none the less evidence that some communities more than held their own. It has been suggested that Brecon underwent continuous growth in the later fourteenth and fifteenth centuries as the *caput* of a major lordship situated on the main through route from England to west Wales. The ranks of its *burgesses* increased in the period after 1400. Carmarthen's position was sustained by its administrative role as capital of the southern Principality, as well as its port and markets, which were becoming dominant in the south west. Ruthin, too, may have weathered the period well, developing its clothmaking and shoemaking industries.

Almost certainly, though, the later Middle Ages brought problems for the smaller medieval foundations, and for boroughs that, like Holt, were poorly placed once the political and military reasons for their existence were cut away. We should probably think of this period as one of rationalization of markets, a rationalization that continued for the major part of the century that was to follow. Indeed, there are signs that the early sixteenth century brought renewed problems connected to the readjustments underway in the agrarian economy and inland and overseas trade. If this was so, then we may be justified in regarding this as a period of urban crisis comparable to that suggested in the case of the much larger English provincial towns. Apart from the evidence of John *Leland*, who was hardly flattering about many of the Welsh boroughs, there are two acts of Parliament dating from the 1540s which are especially suggestive. One, of 1543, was an act 'for the making of *friezes* and
C.15 cottons in Wales' (C.15). It suggests that contemporaries had identified several problems in the west Wales boroughs and

attributed them to a relocation of the clothing industry in the countryside, free of the restrictive practices (and quality controls) of the urban craft guilds. Many English towns in which the textile industry was an important employer and source of trade suffered from exactly the same phenomenon in this period. The second act, passed in the following session, 'for the repairing and
C.16 amending of certain decayed towns and tenements' (C.16) was one of a series of acts in the later Parliaments of Henry VIII aimed at renewing the urban fabric throughout the nation. Some confusion has arisen over this legislation, for amongst the Welsh towns identified as in need of repair were some, such as New Radnor, which had already shrunk profoundly and irrecoverably, and others, such as Cardiff, Swansea and Carmarthen, which were amongst the most populous boroughs. Certainly the inclusion of Cardiff in this list does not immediately square with *Merrick*'s attractive description of the town's condition a
C.17 generation later (C.17). We should not assume, however, that those who had pressed for this legislation had the foresight to recognize the fact that for some towns no recovery was likely or possible. More to the point is that a common symptom of urban contraction had been called to the attention of Members of Parliament.

Corroborative evidence is available to a degree. First, we know ourselves from contemporary documentation, of decayed *burgage plots* in many towns — though, as noted above, we are less sure of the significance of this fact. Secondly, that there was a decline, for example, in Carmarthen's clothing industry, is reflected in the effort made by the borough corporation to revive it in the 1570s. In 1574 new charters were granted to the moribund weavers' and *tuckers' guilds* as part of a complete overhaul of the town's fraternities and a reform of the quality of manufactures. The same period saw new charters granted to guilds in Haverfordwest, perhaps for the same reason. Moreover, there is additional evidence for severe difficulties in Tenby and Pembroke during this century. Owen's account of fairs and markets in his native county suggests that for Pembroke — the
C.18 county town — no solution to this crisis had been found (C.18). The lesser west Wales boroughs as a group had first of all to come to terms with the fact that Carmarthen and Haverfordwest were

better placed as centres of inland trade. They had advantages, too, as maritime communities, advantages of location, and of suitable berthing for vessels. Tenby suffered in particular from the concentration of overseas trade on Carmarthen and Haverfordwest. This was part of a general realignment of overseas links with Welsh ports in the Tudor period.

In the later Middle Ages and early sixteenth century the northern port of Beaumaris and Haverfordwest, Pembroke, Tenby, Carmarthen, Swansea and Cardiff, all had strong international connections. Beaumaris lost this role by the 1560s as French vessels, drawn by the coal export trade, concentrated their activity in the waters of the Bristol Channel. Breton merchants and ships came to focus in particular on Swansea, Neath, Carmarthen and Milford Haven, bringing into Wales cargoes of salt and luxuries such as wine, taking home coal, cloth, hides, corn and butter. Tenby seems to have suffered from a loss of its continental trade at an early stage; by Elizabeth's reign its extramural suburb was thoroughly decayed and there were serious gaps in the streets within the walls. *Leland*'s comment that the town was 'very wealthy by merchandise' is rather misleading. By the end of the sixteenth century a new balance was being struck in the region which fuelled a recovery of prosperity in the borough. Tenby concentrated now on a more local trade with Ireland, with Bristol and the harbours of the west country, and with Cardigan Bay. In much the same fashion, the north Wales ports of Caernarfon and Beaumaris lost their ties with Bristol, and became intimately linked instead with Chester and Liverpool.

Tenby's recovery was not solely a function of a relocation of trade. The later sixteenth century witnessed a dramatic growth in coastal and cross-channel trade. It is easy to be influenced by impressionistic evidence for the well-being of the Welsh port
C.19 towns before this date. Phaer's report (C.19) is a helpful source of information on their connections; it also reminds us that they had to compete with a host of creeks and harbours that were not linked to any borough. What statistical material we have suggests the absence of a well-developed ship-owning and mercantile sector before the later years of the century. In the 1560s Caernarfon ports possessed no ships of their own, while the five

Carmarthenshire ports mustered a total of 40 sailors and eight ships totalling 143 tons, only one of which was fit for foreign service. English and Breton vessels, masters and merchants dominated. By the end of the century, however, increasing population and demand for the products of Welsh agriculture involved larger numbers of Welshmen and ships in trade by sea, enabling Owen, in the 1590s to comment of Pembrokeshire that 'this country is much fallen to trade by sea'. By this date, however, trade had concentrated into fewer points, and the losers in west Wales, amongst the more important medieval towns, were Pembroke and Kidwelly.

By 1600 also there is evidence that a comparable expansion of inland trade was likewise contributing to a renaissance of town life. This is less easy to quantify, and much of the evidence is circumstantial. Population figures are not much help. They suggest at best a picture of uneven growth. Caernarfon's population may have more than doubled in size between 1550 and 1670, as did Wrexham's, outstripping Carmarthen to become
C.20 the largest Welsh town (C.20). Population growth is, however, no more an index of prosperity than is contraction of population, although the steep decline of Kidwelly from a population of 1,200 or so in 1550, to around 600 a century later, corroborates other evidence for the slide of the community. Increasing population could be a source of social problems as much as a function of increased trade. More interesting is the evidence that the later sixteenth and early seventeenth centuries saw attempts to revive failed or moribund markets and the building of new market halls. In some cases — Kidwelly or Grosmont, for instance — such schemes to attract a share of expanding internal trade met with little success. In others, new charters and new domestic and corporate building genuinely reflect a new-found health. In England as well this was a period which saw a revival in the fortunes of the smaller market towns with which most Welsh centres compared. *Jacobean* consumers could take advantage of a much wider range of commodities for sale than could their predecessors and gradually improving communications enabled some, if not all, towns to benefit from the growth in demand and spending power. Political changes — the creation of *burgess* Members of Parliament, of *Great Sessions* and *Quarter*

*Sessions* — and the expansion of grammar schooling assisted in this by attracting wealthy gentlemen and *yeomen* into the towns.

By the early seventeenth century, too, there were signs of a growing specialization in marketing within the urban sector of the Welsh economy, though this only becomes clear after the *Restoration.* Knighton, for example, developed a reputation for fruits and hops; Dolgellau and Welshpool for cloth. The livestock trade ensured that certain well-located towns, through their markets and fairs, acted as vital channels in the exchange of goods and services with England, despite the expansion of rural fairs and private bargaining. In the reign of James I the largest and healthiest Welsh towns, in *the Marches* and on the coasts, looked outward towards England and were increasingly integrated into English regional economies. Smaller local market centres — those that had survived an age of winnowing — were at the same time, it seems, experiencing at least a temporary boom.

It was in these ways that growth in the countryside, and the social changes this brought about, had, by the end of the Tudor period, inaugurated a growth in town life. At present we can only sketch in the general contours of these developments — and we are far less secure in our understanding of Welsh urban history under the Tudors than we are in our knowledge of agrarian change. Detailed information on urban social and occupational structures, and on the activity of markets becomes available only in the seventeenth century. More than ever, local studies have a major role in developing a more sophisticated understanding of the chronology of change in both rural and urban society.

## Sources

C.1 They have begun of late to lime their land
And ploughs the ground where sturdy oaks did stand,
Converts the meres and marrish everywhere . . .
They tear up trees and take the roots away,
Makes stony fields smooth fertile fallow ground,
Brings pastures bare to bear good grass for hay . . .
Wales is this day (behold throughout the shires)
In better state than 'twas this hundred years.

(Thomas Churchyard, *The Worthines of Wales*, 1587).

C.2

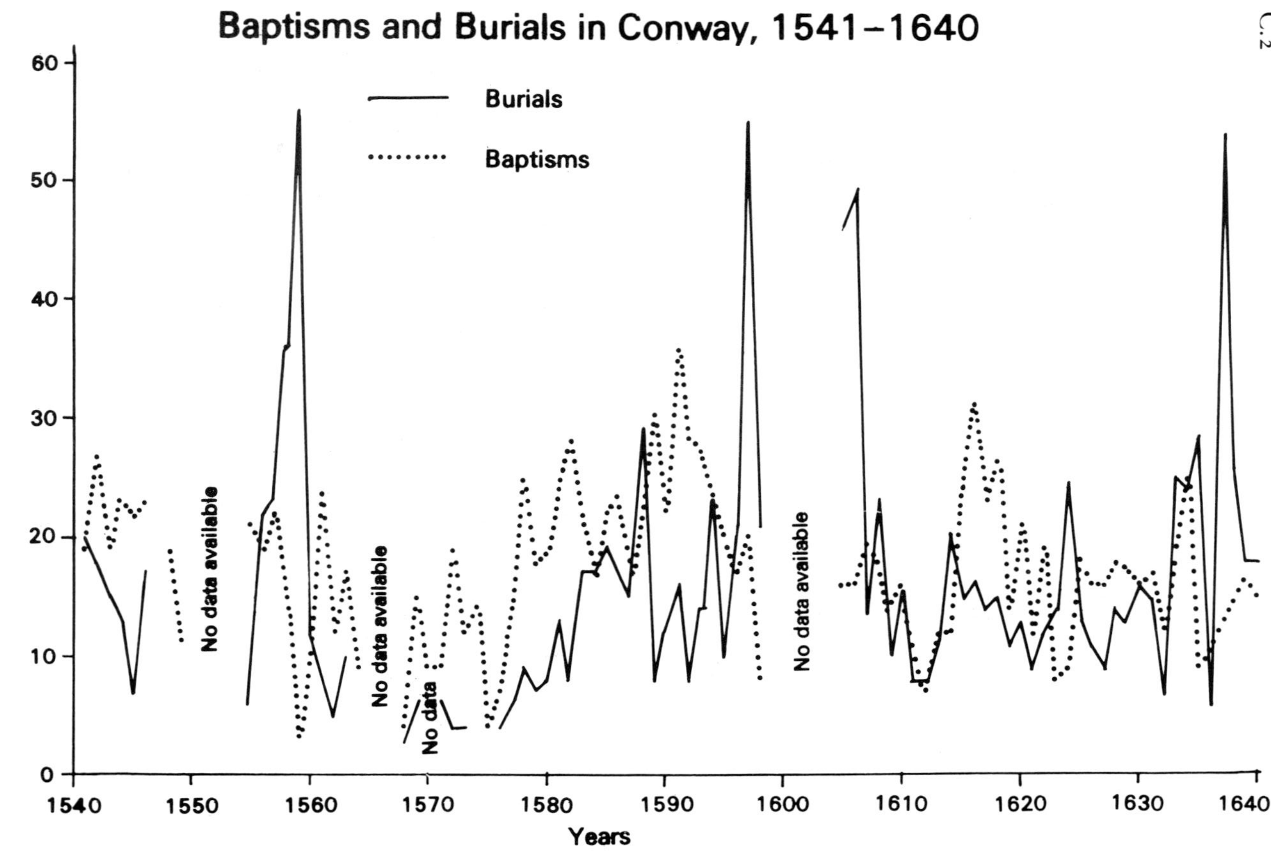
Baptisms and Burials in Conway, 1541–1640
Burials
Baptisms
60
50
40
30
20
10
0
No data available
No data available
No data
No data available
1540
1550
1560
1570
1580
1590
1600
1610
1620
1630
1640
Years

C.3

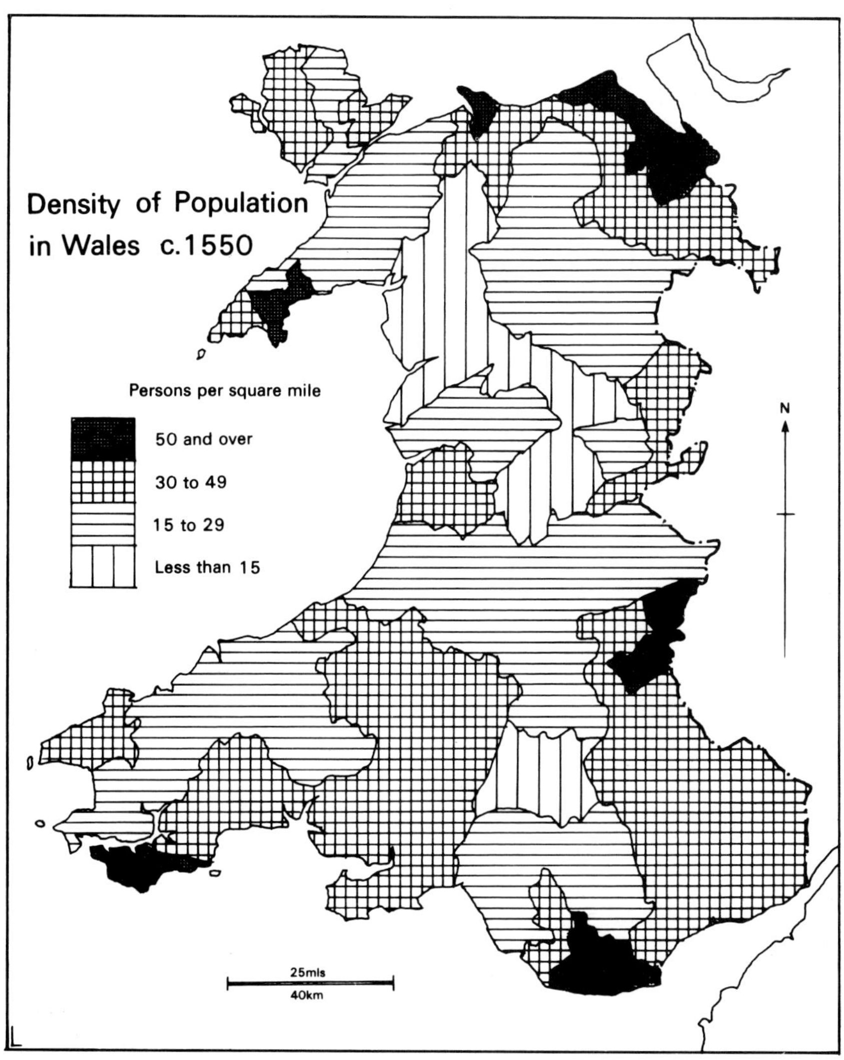
Density of Population
in Wales c.1550
Persons per square mile
50 and over
30 to 49
15 to 29
Less than 15
N
25mls
40km

C.4

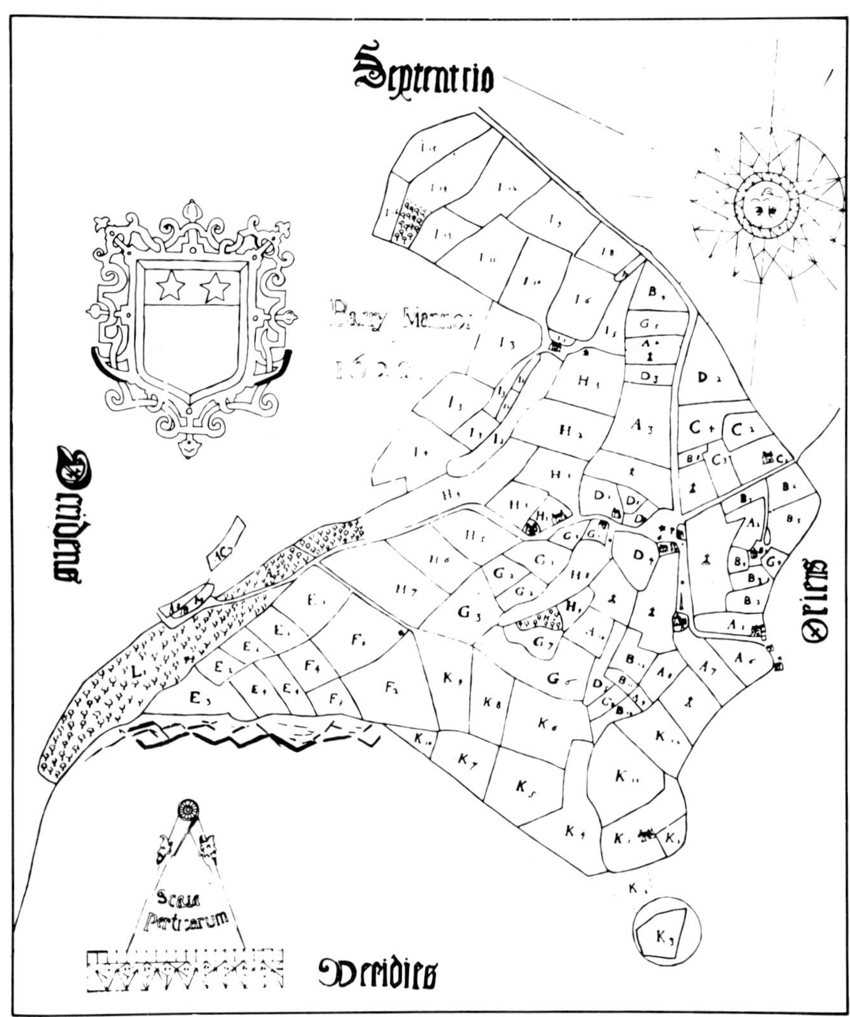


Map of Barry Manor in 1622 by Evans Mouse, based on original in Glamorgan Record Office. (*Source: H.J. Evans.*)

C.5 This part of the country was always renowned as well for the fertility of the soil, and abundance of all things serving to the necessity or pleasure of man, as also for the temperature and wholesomeness of the air. And was a champion and open country, without great store of inclosures; for in my time old men reported that they remembered in their youth that cattle in some time, for want of shade, to have from the Port Wat run to Barry, which is four miles distant, whose forefathers told them that great part of the inclosures was made in their days.

(Rice Merrick, *Morganiae archaiographia*, ed. Brian Ll. James, Barry 1983, p.14. Merrick began his account of Glamorgan in about 1578).

C.6 Whereas most of the land in these two counties consists of mountains, hills and other waste ground on which the freeholders have had as far back as can be remembered common of pasture all the year round so breeding yearly great numbers of horses, mares and geldings as well for the maintenance of the strength of the Realm as for the upkeep of tillage; also no small number of oxen, kine, sheep and other cattle for food. Yet divers persons within these counties preferring their private lucre and gain before the welfare of the country, have within the last twenty years or so acquired cottages and other small freeholds and do in the summer put on the mountains and hills not only their own cattle but also cattle hired from other men, making such number of cattle as the hill pasture will scarce suffice to feed for half the summer . . .
4. It was not lawful for any freeholder or his undertenant within the said lordships marcher to erect any cottage or hovel without the lord's licence . . . (before they were made shire ground)
5. It was not lawful for any freeholder to dwell in any cottage or hovel so made but from 15th of May to 15th of August, if he did contrary he was fined . . .

(Petition to the President of the Council of the Marches, from Edward Herbert and James Price, esquires, and 'most of the freeholders in the counties of Montgomery and Radnor'. From Ralph Flenley (ed.), *A Calendar of the Register of the Council in the Marches of Wales*, Cymmrodorion Record Series, 8, 1916, pp.105-7. The petition can be dated to November 1573).

C.7 To the right honourable Sir William Cecil, knight, Lord Burghley, Lord High Treasurer of England and Master of Her Majesty's Court of Wards and Liveries . . . whereas the right honourable William, late earl of Worcester . . . was in his life time seized in his demesne as of fee tail of an estate . . . in one pasture called the *Bantwayne* containing by estimation twelve acres; one meadow called *Gweine y Lleverith* containing by estimation thirty acres; and of and in one tenement and certain lands thereunto belonging now in the occupation of John Landegg; one parcel of lands called *Tree Boyth* containing about twenty and six acres now in the occupation of one George Franklin, being parcels of the manor of *Tryvyddva* . . . and also of and in one close called *Malefante's Cloase* with divers other lands sometime one David Mallefante's and now in the occupation of one John Russell. And also of and in divers parcels of wastes and waste grounds now reduced into several and lately encroached, drawn in and enclosed from and out of the *demesnes* call Oystermouth Moor and Clyne Forest, being parcels and members of the manor of Oystermouth . . . and also of and in certain lands and tenements commonly called *Burryeshead* containing about three hundred acres of meadow, pasture and arable in the several occupations of Henry Manxell, gentleman, Philip Bowen, gentleman, Thomas Franklin, gentleman and Robert Smith, *yeoman* . . .

(Bill of complaint exhibited in the Court of Wards on behalf of the Queen and Edward earl of Worcester, 1590. From W.R.B. Robinson, 'The litigation of Edward, earl of Worcester concerning Gower 1590–96' (part 1), *Bulletin of the Board of Celtic Studies*, XXII, 1966–8, pp.171–2).

C.8 One other cause (why winter corn was not sown) was the use of *gavelkind* used among most of these Welshmen to part all the father's patrimony among all his sons, so that in process of time the whole country was brought into small pieces of ground and intermingled up and down one with another, so as in every five or six acres you shall have ten or twelve owners. This made the country to remain champion and without enclosures or hedging. And winter corn, if it were sown among them, should be grazed all the winter and eaten by sheep and other cattle which could not be kept from the same . . . This in my opinion was one chief cause they restrained sowing of winter corn, but as now since the use of *gavelkind* is abolished for these threescore years past, in many parts the ground is brought together by purchase and exchanges, and hedging and enclosures much increased, and now they fall to the tilling of this winter corn in greater abundance than before.

(George Owen, *The Description of Penbrockshire*, 1603, ed. Henry Owen, I, 1892, p.61).

C.9

Aerial photograph New Radnor, 1967. (*Source: University of Cambridge, Committee for Aerial Photography.*)

C.10 Distribution of Wealth, Caernarfonshire, Subsidy of 34–35 Henry VIII. Ranked in Order of Wealth.

| *Commote*/ Borough | Total Capital Value | Acres (excl. water) | Pence/ Acre |
|---|---|---|---|
| Caernarvon | £640 | 1,897 | 81.0 |
| Conway | £123-10-0 | 700 | 42.34 |
| Gafflogion | £526 | 11,334 | 11.13 |
| Cymydmaen | £709 | 25,240 | 6.7 |
| Eifionydd | £839 | 46,070 | 4.37 |
| Isgwrfai | £714 | 40,869 | 4.19 |
| Creuddyn & Isaf | £550 | 35,419 | 3.73 |
| Dinllaen | £433-10-0 | 28,992 | 3.6 |
| Nantconwy | £600 | 46,326 | 3.1 |
| Uchaf | £450-10-0 | 47,950 | 2.25 |
| Uwchfwrfai | £584-10-0 | 64,238 | 2.2 |
| Whole shire | £6,170 | 338,135 | 4.4 |
| Whole shire, excl. Conway & Caernarvon | £5,406-10-0 | 336,238 | 3.86 |

(Royston Stephens, 'Gwynedd 1528–1547. Economy and Society in Tudor Wales', U.C.L.A. Ph.D. Diss. 1975).

C.11 John Leland (1536–9)
*New Radnor*

. . . hath been metely well walled, and in the walls appear the ruins of our gates. There is an old church standing now as a chapel by the castle; not very far thence is the new parish church . . . The building of the town is in some part metely good, in most part but rude, many houses being thatched. The castle is in ruin, but that a piece of the gate was a late (*sic*) amended. The town was defaced in Henry the fourth days by *Owyn Glyndŵr*.

(Lucy Toulmin Smith (ed.), *The Itinerary in Wales of John Leland*, 1906, p.10).

*Presteigne*

. . . a very good market of corn, to the which many folks of Melenith resort to buy corn, and beside is no notable building in the lordship of Presteigne.

(Ibid, p.10).

*Knighton*

. . . a pretty town after the Welsh building . . .

(Ibid, pp.10–11).

*Dinefwr*

Here was sometime a long street now ruinous.

(Ibid, p.59).

*Kidwelly*

There is a little town now but newly made between Gwendraeth Fawr and Gwendraeth Fechan rivers but hard on Gwendraeth Fechan. Gwendraeth Fawr is half a mile off. There is betwixt New Kidwelly and the Old but a bridge over little Gwendraeth. The old town is prettily walled and hath hard by the wall a castle. The old town is near all desolated, but the castle is meetly well kept up. It belonged to the Duke of Lancaster. In the new town is only a Church of Our Lady, and by is the cell of the Black Monks of Sherbourne. There the Prior is parson of Our Lady Church. I saw three gates, and over one of them was the ruin of a fair town hall, and under, a prison. A piece of the new town was lately burned. The new town is three times as big as the old. Since the haven of Gwendraeth Fechan decayed, the new town is sore decayed. Carmarthen hath increased since Kidwelly haven decayed.

(Ibid, p.58).

*Denbigh*

The town and castle of Denbigh standeth on a craggy hill, and is near a mile in compass . . . The castle lieth south of the town; and the town lieth to the castle by north and east. In the town be but two gates, the Exchequer Gate and the *Burgess* Gate. In the first was the lord's court kept; and in the other the *Burgesses'*. The Exchequer Gate lieth plain west, and the *Burgesses'* Gate plain north . . . There hath been divers rows of streets within the walled town, of which the most part be now down in manner, and at this time there be scant eighty householders. There is a goodly and large chapel of ease in the old town, of St Hilary, whither yet most of the new town yet come. I have not yet learned the certainty how this walled town decayed within, whether it were by fire or for lack of water, whereof there is little or none, or for lack of good carriage into the town standing somewhat high on rocky ground, I cannot surely tell. But the town of Denbigh now occupied and joining near to the old town hath been totally made of later time and set much more to commodity of carriage and water by many wells in it. And the increase of this was the decay of the other. At the present time the new is three times as big as the old . . . and in the market place well builded, which is fair and large, and paved of late years, the confluence to the market on Tuesday is exceeding great.

(Ibid, pp.96–7).

C.12 William Camden (1586)

*Builth*

Builth is a town pleasantly seated, with woods about it, and fortified with a castle . . . At present tis noted for a good market.

(William Camden, *Britannia*, 1586; cited in 1695 edition, p.597).

*Chepstow*

Tis a town of good note, built on a hill close by the river, guarded with walls of a considerable circumference, which take in several fields and orchards. The castle is very fair, standing on the brink of a river; and on the opposite side there stood a priory whereof the better part being demolished, the remainder is converted to a parish church. The bridge over the Wye is built upon piles, and is exceeding high, which was necessary, because the tide rises here to a great height.

(Ibid, p.597).

*Tenby*

A neat town, and strongly walled, beholds the sea from the dry shore; a place much noted for the ships that harbour there, and for plenty of fish, whence in British it is called *Dinbech y Pyskod*; governed by a Mayor and Bailiff.

(Ibid, p.622).

*Caernarfon*

This town is encompassed with a firm wall, though of a small circumference; and shows a beautiful castle, which takes up all the west side of it. The private buildings, for the manner of the country, are neat; and the civility of the inhabitants much commended.

(Ibid, p.666).

C.13

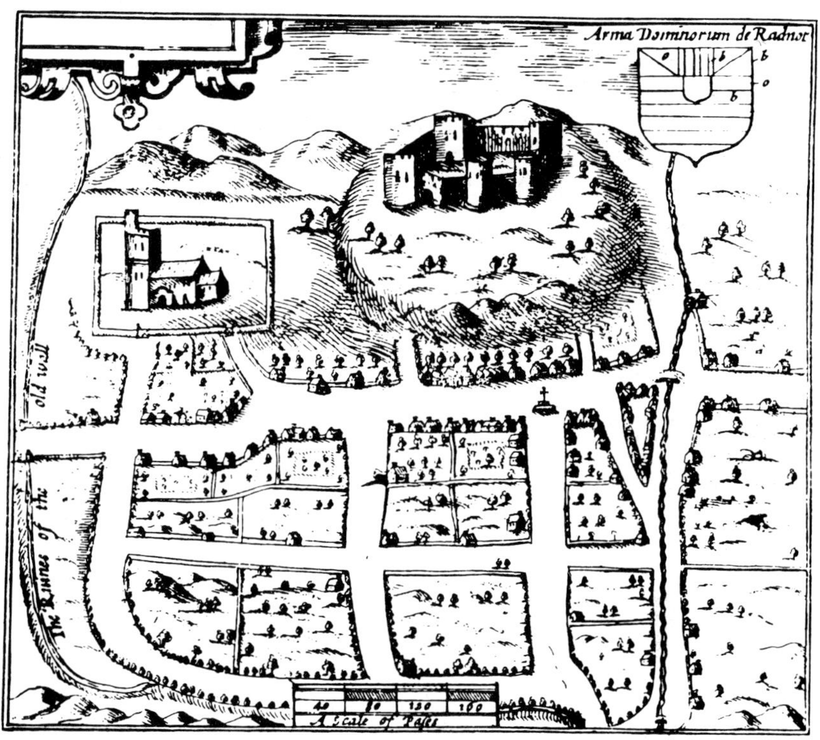


New Radnor in the early seventeenth century; map published in John Speed's *Theatre of the Empire of Great Britain*, 1611.

C.14

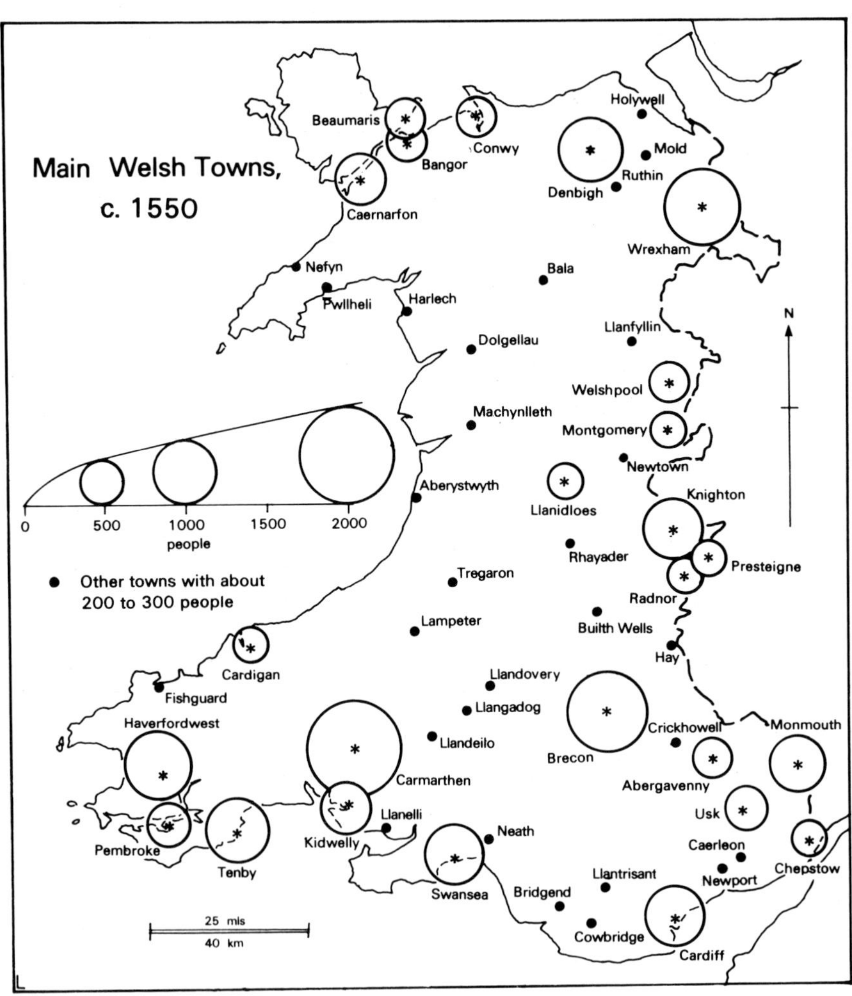
Main Welsh Towns, c. 1550
0
500
1000
1500
2000
people
Other towns with about 200 to 300 people
25 mls
40 km
N
Beaumaris
Bangor
Conwy
Caernarfon
Holywell
Mold
Ruthin
Denbigh
Wrexham
Nefyn
Pwllheli
Harlech
Bala
Llanfyllin
Dolgellau
Welshpool
Montgomery
Machynlleth
Newtown
Aberystwyth
Llanidloes
Knighton
Rhayader
Presteigne
Radnor
Tregaron
Lampeter
Builth Wells
Hay
Cardigan
Fishguard
Llandovery
Llangadog
Haverfordwest
Llandeilo
Brecon
Crickhowell
Monmouth
Carmarthen
Abergavenny
Usk
Llanelli
Kidwelly
Neath
Caerleon
Chepstow
Pembroke
Tenby
Swansea
Bridgend
Llantrisant
Newport
Cowbridge
Cardiff

C.15 For as much as the inhabitants, clothmakers that dwell within the towns and boroughs of Carmarthenshire, Cardiganshire and Pembrokeshire have used in the past to make their cloth called Welsh *frieze* and cotton called Welsh cotton . . . which true and good making of *friezes* hath been of long time decayed and extinguished, and yet is, to the great decay and ruin of all the said towns and boroughs . . . and the principal occasion is that the clothiers, tuckers and weavers . . . that were wont to inhabit within the said towns and boroughs . . . be now become foreigners, *husbandmen* and graziers dwelling in the country . . . and there do make their own wool, *friezes* and cottons.

(Act for the making of Friezes and Cottons in Wales, from *Statutes of the Realm*, III, p.909: 34 & 5 Henry VIII, c.xi).

C.16 Forasmuch as in times past diverse and many beautiful houses of habitation have been within the walls and liberties of the [towns of Shrewsbury, Chester, Ludlow, Haverfordwest, Pembroke, Tenby, Carmarthen, Montgomery, Cardiff, Swansea, Cowbridge, New Radnor, Presteigne, Brecon, Monmouth, Maldon (Essex), Abergavenny, Usk, Caerleon, Newport, Lancaster, Preston, Liverpool, and Wigan] . . . which now are fallen down, decayed and at this time remain unre-edified, lying as desolate and void grounds, and many of them adjoining nigh unto the high streets, replenished with much other filth and uncleanness, with pits, cellars, and vaults lying open and uncovered . . . to the decay and hindrance of the said city and boroughs and towns.

(Act 'Touching the repairing and amending of certain decayed houses and tenements', from *Statutes of the Realm*, 35 Henry c.iv: p.959).

C.17 *Cardiff* (*c.*1578)
This town, for the most part, is environed with a fair high wall, garreted, and place thereon to walk, saving where the river Taff and the tide, undermining it, overturned part thereof, in compass about a mile. In the north part of the town standeth a fair castle, called the castle of Cardiff, the ward wall of the castle severing them. Upon this town [wall] are four fair gates (besides the castle

gate and other posterns) in the four quarters thereof. The first in the east part, therefore called the East Gate; the second in the west commonly called the West or Miskin Gate; the third in the north, therefore called the North or Senghennydd Gate; the fourth in the south called the South Gate, near unto the quay. On the town wall was builded a tower, called Cock's Tower, to defend the town against the danger of the sea.

Within the town walls are two parish churches. The one called St John's, being a fair church, with two aisles, standing upon bossed and embowed pillars of a fair freestone; and the chancel compassed with two fair aisles. And in the west end a very fair steeple of grey ashlar, with four gates of freestone, very workmanly wrought, standing upon four strong pillars underpropping the same; the workmanship of it, being carried to a great height, and above beautified with pinnacles, of all skilful beholders is very well like of. It was made in *anno Domini* [ . . . ] by [ . . . ] Hart, a mason, who made the towers of Wrexham and of St Stephen's, in Bristol. This church standeth not far from the middle of the town.

The other, called St Mary's church, which is of far greater antiquity, supposed to be of some religion, standeth in the south-west part of the town, the yard whereof reached near the quay, to which also the inhabitants, before that Cardiff was enlarged, as before is said, were parishioners. To this church is annexed the church or chapel of Roath, for therein they have their christening, marriage and burial. The castle of Cardiff standeth within this parish.

Within the town walls were two chapels; the one called the Shoemakers' chapel, being of very high building, yet standeth in Shoemakers' Street; the other hard by the West Gate, now decayed, for a stairs for the castle is now there made.

Without the West Gate was a house of Black Friars, founded by Richard de Clare, Earl of Gloucester and sometime lord of Glamorgan, *anno* 1256. And without the North Gate Gilbert de Clare, being lord of Glamorgan, founded the Grey Friars, wherein Sir William Herbert, knight, hath builded a house of late.

The town is very well compacted, beautified with many fair houses and large streets; it is almost square or quadrant, but more in length from the south toward the north than the other way.

In the chief street, called the High Street, standeth a fair town hall, wherein is holden the town court every fortnight. Adjoining to the same is a fair shambles below, wherein victuals are sold; and above, a fair great chamber, where the aldermen and magistrates use to consult; and under the hall is the prison wherein offenders and misdoers are committed, which is called *Cwchmoel.*

And in the south part of the guildhall is a chamber wherein juries, being sworn, remain; and such as are committed, convict upon executions . . .

In the south part of the guildhall, in the middle of four cross ways, is built a fair cross, quadrant, with joists covered over with lead; under which, and near abouts, is the corn market twice kept weekly, viz. on Wednesday and Saturday.

In the High Street, which extendeth from the guildhall northward toward the castle, being a fair and wide street, is kept market for all other necessaries to be sold, as aforesaid.

Within this town and the liberties thereof are two great fairs kept; viz., the first on St Peter and St Paul's Day, the other on the Nativity of St Mary and St Andrew's Day.

Within this town be many fair and large streets, and buildings accordingly, which I mean not particularly to describe, because I intend to describe it by card.

Within the walls is little or no vacant or waste ground, saving for gardens, and those very small, because it is so well replenished with buildings.

In this town is plenty of good viands to be sold, as well for that it is environed with a plentiful and rich soil, as also for the continual recourse from it by sea to Bristol and other good towns in England . . .

(Rice Merrick, *A Booke of Glamorganshires Antiquities*, ed. James Andrew Corbett, London, 1887, pp.92–6).

C.18a *Fairs and markets in Pembrokeshire*, 1603

I have before declared, that there are three market towns in Pembrokeshire, viz. Pembroke, Haverfordwest and Tenby, the second whereof, being seated in the midst of the shire, and most convenient for trade, is greatly frequented of the country people, and therefore is the greatest, and plentifulest market of the shire, and is kept once every week on the Saturday, wherein methinketh the town is very backward in their own profit, in not suing for another market in the middle of the week, which would turn to the great good both of the town and the country; also they have but one fair in the year, whereas if there were more purchased from His Majesty it would be beneficial both for town and country.

The market of Haverfordwest is thought to be one of the greatest and plentifulest markets (all things compared) that is within the marches of Wales; especially for the plenty and goodness of victual, as namely for beef, mutton, pork, bacon, veal, goose, capon, kid, lamb, coney, turkey, and all sorts of wildfowl in their season, that it is a marvel to many, where the victuals that are there to be seen at noon should be shifted away ere night, and for fish it passeth all others in Wales, without any comparison, both for plenty and variety.

Pembroke market is also on the Saturday, and Tenby on Saturday for victuals, and on Wednesday for corn. These two towns for their markets are much inferior for plenty of victuals and corn to that of Haverfordwest, by reason those towns are seated, the one very near the lower parts of the shire, and much hindered by reason of a ferry on the one side, and Tenby seemeth as it were a town running out of the country, and stayed on the sea cliff by reason whereof they stand not so commodious for resort of people, which maketh less trade and utterance in their markets, but both of these towns being seated in a more fruitful soil than Haverfordwest is, for goodness of victual are nothing inferior, if not better than Haverford, and so for goodness of corn, and for fish especially Tenby, and therefore it is in Welsh called *Denbigh y pyscod* (sic), that is, 'fish Tenby', for difference between it and Denbigh in North Wales. But as these markets are highly to be commended for plenty and goodness of victuals, so hath each of them a great maim of a good market, which being reformed, as easily it might be, would greatly turn to the good of the market and the market men; that is there is no use of sale of live cattle in any of these markets, which is the greatest commendation and commodity of many markets in England, for in these markets there are neither horses, oxen, kine, calves, sheep, lambs, swine, or any other kind of living cattle brought or offered to be sold, so that the poor man wanting money, and having cattle to spare, cannot have money for the same till the summer fairs come, which begin not before the 16 of June, and end in November whereby it cometh to pass that whatsoever the *husbandman* buyeth in the six months of December, January, February, March, April and May, he buyeth all at days to be paid at the fair days, when he may have money for oxen, kine, sheep or lambs, and by this means the rich man eateth up the wealth of the poor man . . . This a mighty inconvenience in the commonwealth of this poor country, and with a little industry of the better sort of people might be redressed, for if they did but begin the use of bringing cattle to the markets, the poor man that wanted money should know where to have money to serve his use, and also those that want either ox, cow, sheep or hog know not where to supply their wants, for want of this use, which I have long wished I might see some good men would enterprize to induce, and no doubt God would prosper the action and all good commonwealth men would commend and further.

There are also markets of victuals used in St David's and Newport not worth the speaking of, partly for that they be so small and bad, but especially for the abuse, for that the same is used every Sunday before service, even about sunrising.

There hath been in times past divers markets used in divers other places, and by reason of the poverty of the towns and the unaptness of the places altogether decayed, as at Cilgerran, Fishguard, St Dogmaels, Rosemarket, Wiston, Llawhaden, where, by report of ancient men, markets have been kept in old time.

Also it appeareth that there hath been a great market at Newport every Thursday, as well by toll received from the same as also by a fair deed yet extant, which passed between the lord of the manor, and all his tenants and freeholders of Cemais in Edward I's time, whereby they bind them and their heirs, and tenants, not to sell anything, but first to offer the same to be sold at the market of Newport; and there to pay toll for the same, but now there is no use of this, nor any market there, which among other things I suppose to have been the chiefest cause of the decay of that town.

(George Owen, *The Description of Penbrockshire*, ed. H Owen, vol.I, London, 1892, pp.140–2).

C.18b Also your towns are not as the rest of the towns of Wales are; you are more English like in all points to the English towns. When I came to the fine town of Tenby I wondered to see the people whom I found so full of courtesy and kindness towards me a stranger that it made me to admire. Rich and poor, young and old, yielded me reverence, entertained me, invited me, accompanied me, because I was a stranger. Truly it is one of the finest little towns and inhabited with best people that ever I came in. And your ancient shire town of Pembroke though now greatly decayed yet still doth it carry the show of a good town, loving people and courteous, very civil and orderly. The decay of that town being the head of your shire and which was in such estimation as it hath been in your country in times past made my heart sorry, and for your good town of Haverfordwest, I never came into a town of better entertainment nor where I was better fed; very civil people. I could not imagine that I was then in Wales. It seemeth that that town of Haverfordwest is a very thriving town, and many townsmen of good wealth which doubtless they well deserve, God continue his blessings among them. It seemeth that your country of Pembrokeshire is a bigger shire when these towns are well maintained.

(George Owen, *The Dialogue of the Government of Wales*, 1594, ed. H. Owen, vo.I, London, 1892).

C.19 Chepstow, a haven of three fathoms at low water somewhat dangerous to come to, for rocks called the *Shootes*. It lieth over against Aust in Gloucestershire. All westerly and southerly winds brings in. The town of Chepstow and country adjoining meetly well furnished of all manner victuals and other provision.

Cardiff, from Newport 12 miles. A proper town walled where is a dry haven. And without the same is a road in Severn called Penarth, very good for ships at three fathom low water. It lieth against Axewater and Bridgwater in Somerset . . . The towns of Cardiff and Cowbridge adjoining replenished with corn and all manner victualls.

Carmarthen an ancient town well traded and peopled, where there is an old castle of the king's in the keeping of my lord of Pembroke . . . And here is great passage of leather, tallow and hides by reason of the merchants. All this country is very bare of corn and not able to live of their own provision, for the most part of their tillage is oats, and are served of wheat and malt out of the Forest of Dean and other parts. Laugharne and Llanstephan be two poor towns upon the said haven . . .

The haven of Milford lieth against Padstow in Cornwall . . . Here is great transporting to Ireland of corn and money and many other things without controllment, for men may do what they will ere they be spied by the officer and pass when they please by reason of the haven being so large and secret.

Aberystwyth, from Cardigan 24 miles. A barred haven of no value. The mayor of the town claimeth the port. All this a very bare country and mountains. At Aberystwyth is a castle of the king's decayed but the hall remaineth yet covered with lead. Here it is to be noted that from St David's Head all along this coast is no trade of merchandise but all full of rocks and dangers.

Beaumaris . . . a goodly haven and a road for all ships. Beaumaris itself being the chief town of the isle. A proper town and a strong castle.

*Memorandum* that the isle of Anglesey is in length direct 22 miles and 14 broad, well inhabited, abundant of corn, cattle and all good provision except wood, good trade of merchandise and many gentelmen.

From Nefyn 16 miles to Caernarfon, a barred haven for a ship of a 100 [tons] at a spring. The town of Caernarfon well inhabited where the king's majesty hath a strong castle.

Between Nefyn and Caernarfon is a little bay called White Bay, to no great purpose but for the fishing of salmons, whereof in the summer they have great plenty. From Caernarfon 10 mile to Penrhyn and Bangor, a barred haven serving for nothing but to lead slates.

Conway from thence 12 miles. A good barred haven for 100 ton where there is a town and a goodly fair castle of the king's majesty's.

(From W.R.B. Robinson, 'Dr Thomas Phaer's report on the harbours and customs administration of Wales under Edward VI', *Bulletin of the Board of Celtic Studies*, xxiv, 1970–2, pp.485–503).

## Debating the Evidence

Once more historians rely on similar kinds of sources to those used in other sections to provide information about life in Welsh countryside and town in Tudor times. One preconception to be rid of is that of the twentieth-century town. The size of Tudor towns compares with that of our villages. And the balance of town location within Wales has changed out of all recognition. The south Wales coastal cities of Swansea, Cardiff and Newport are the creations of an economic change of the nineteenth century — industrialization. Additionally, as Matthew Griffiths points out in his article, the *inter-relationship* between countryside and town was wholly different from that which pertains today.

*Source C.1*

How might Thomas Churchyard have been in a position to comment on the scale of change in Wales over the previous hundred years? Does Churchyard's comment on economic change tally with that made by *George Owen* about social and political transformation (A.17)? Do you think that the two categories of change are inter-related? Were political peace and full administrative integration into England a precondition of economic growth?

*Source C.2*

The study of demography, or population change, is extremely complex for the Tudor period. Specialists say that it is impossible to obtain accurate figures from the sources available, though it is often possible to identify trends. What help do you think estimates like this might be for the historian if they are not absolutely accurate? What might they tell us about (a) disease, (b) the quality of harvests?

*Source C.3*
On the basis of this map what generalizations are we able to make about the population of Wales in Tudor times?

*Source C.5*
What information would you like to have about *Rice Merrick* before accepting this description of part of Glamorgan? What does he mean by 'champion country'?

*Source C.6*
Do you think the cottagers referred to preferred 'their private lucre and gain before the welfare of the country'? What might be the incentives to more intensive pastoral agriculture? And what were its social consequences, according to these passages?

*Source C.7*
What specialist terms would you need to comprehend before being able to make good use of this extract? Where might you go for guidance on their meaning? What interest attaches to the place names in this passage? How far do its comments on enclosure confirm those made in C.5?

*Source C.8*
Is there any evidence in Gwynfor Jones's essay on the gentry which would cast doubt on some of the points which *George Owen* makes here? What relationship does *George Owen* perceive between inheritance, customs, agricultural practice and land usage? Does his attitude towards *gavelkind* highlight his own prejudices?

*Sources C.9/C.13*
What are the similarities and differences between these as sources for the historian?

*Source C.11*
What other kinds of evidence might help to corroborate these descriptions by *John Leland*? Why do you think that *Leland*'s descriptions are so frequently quoted? What takes his eye in the description of a town? Does the fact that he compares one town with another (Carmarthen and Kidwelly) or past and present (Denbigh) enhance the value of his reports?

*Source C.12*
What do these descriptions tell us about *William Camden*'s priorities as he journeyed in Wales?

*Source C.15*
This is part of an Act of Parliament. It is the preamble to the Act. Is there anything in this source on the decline of wool production which leads you to suspect that the account is not objective?

*Sources C.16 and C.17*
If we are doing research on the state of the town of Cardiff in Tudor times, what difficulties are we presented with by using these two documentary extracts in conjunction? What image of Cardiff does the description in C.17 provide? How far is it possible to reconstruct a picture of Elizabethan Cardiff, its economic life and distinguishing features from the descriptions?

*Source C.18a/b*
In what way might it make a difference to our assessment of these documents to know that *George Owen* was a Pembrokeshire man? What further information about him and his work would help us in our use of them? What can be deduced from C.18A about (a) the marketing network of Elizabethan Pembrokeshire, (b) the decay of older market towns and the reasons behind it, and (c) the role of market towns in the local economy?

*Source C.19*
What basically interests Thomas Phaer? Are his descriptions of trade and economic enterprise too generalized to be useful? What other sources might be used to supplement them? Is there any way in which factual topographical accounts such as this might be misleading?

## Discussion

It will be apparent by now that there are very few topics in the study of Tudor Wales on which *George Owen* of Henllys is not one of our major sources (C.8). The Tudor period saw many changes — in government, society, the economy and religious practice. One important change which emerges implicitly in the sources rather than explicitly in the essays is the existence of that body of antiquaries who are so strongly represented in the sources section on *Country and Town*. Four of them, all of whose work is represented in this set of sources, were of particular importance for our knowledge of Tudor Wales. *John Leland* was the Royal Antiquary to King Henry VIII who required him to journey the length and the breadth of England and Wales recording the major features of the countryside, geographical features and buildings particularly (C.11, C.18a, C.18b). *Leland*'s journeys in Wales took place in those crucial years of 1536 to 1539, but his descriptions remain remarkably passive in tone. *Leland* 's work for the early Tudor period is complemented by that of *William Camden* fifty years later (C.12). There were some outstanding Welsh topographers/scholars too. The two most important represented here are *George Owen* and *Rice Merrick*. *George Owen* was, as we have seen, a Pembrokeshire gentleman. *Rice Merrick* was from Glamorgan. He was a member of the gentry class, inevitably, because, as we have seen, it was the class which benefitted from the educational revolution of the Tudor period as more and more lay families flocked to the universities and Inns of Court. He was a scholar and humanist, one who testified to that spirit of intellectual enquiry and interest which exploited to the full the new opportunities of the sixteenth century and which we call Humanism. He was part of a significant change in the development of history as a study. Like *Leland* and *Owen* he was far less concerned with the myths which had dominated people's notions of Welsh history in the Middle Ages, much more concerned with evidence. It was not yet a concern which resulted in the carefully compiled footnotes and bibliographies of present day scholarly works — that was a development which did not take place until the nineteenth century. However, *Merrick*'s concern for evidence was not only a question of meticulous observation. He consulted the work of his predecessors, including *John Leland*, his fellow Welsh scholars, Humphrey Lhuyd and Sir John Price, he read all the historical manuscripts which he could find at the homes of his fellow gentry and he also accumulated oral evidence from the older inhabitants of Glamorgan. The last of these perhaps reminds us that there are few techniques in the study of history which are new! As a result of the work of these antiquaries and mapmakers, like *Speed*, working early in the seventeenth century, we are able for the first time to begin to get a clear visual and descriptive view of Wales and especially its towns. And there are other sources, such as port-books, recording the passage of ships and their cargoes to and from the Welsh ports, which help supplement antiquarians' views.

It would seem, then, that the contemporary evidence for Tudor country and town is just what we would require, with its relative richness, its stress on careful observation, its detail and its comprehensiveness. Again, it would seem particularly beneficial that its antiquarian nature, its emphasis on recording buildings, churches, markets and the like is precisely what we need to build up an objective picture. In fact, even evidence of the kind we have here is not neutral. Churchyard, *Owen*, *Merrick* and *Camden* were selective in what they recorded. The stress in *Leland*'s writings is a particularly obvious one — he is impressed by the frequency and scale of gentry residences. *Rice Merrick* as a Glamorgan man, is likely to be biased in favour of his native county (C.5, C.17). *George Owen* is wrong to imply that it is only since the *Acts of Union* that the disintegrative process of *gavelkind* had been neutralized and larger parcels of land, or estates, had emerged (C.8). So, even when, as with these documents, meticulous observation appears to be paramount, the evidence has to be interpreted and questions asked about its reliability and bias. Even so, the evidence of Tudor writers and map-makers is invaluable in allowing us to build up a picture of the economy and topography of town and country in Tudor times.

# *Religion and Belief*

GLANMOR WILLIAMS

Life was hard and precarious enough for most people in Wales at the beginning of the sixteenth century. Earning their living by backbreaking toil in poor pastoral farming, they were very much at the mercy of the climate, a grudging upland soil, and the many and frequent outbreaks of diseases which could afflict them and their livestock. Yet their religion taught them that they could secure protection against the demons and evil spirits by which they believed themselves to be surrounded and make their peace with God only through his Church and its ministers, or else their life in the world to come would be infinitely worse and more painful than in this one. Condemned sinners would find that after the Last Judgement their existence would be an eternity of unspeakable torment in Hell. Small wonder, therefore, that their chief concern was to try to find some security for themselves against the terrors of the hereafter by means of the good offices of priests and saints, pilgrimages and shrines, penance and
D.1 pardon (D.1).

A profound restlessness, nevertheless, prevailed among some unsatisfied souls. From 1517 onwards, a religious revolutionary of genius, Martin Luther, voiced not only the doubts which assailed many but also propounded a confident answer to them based on his own experience. He proclaimed that it was a believer's own faith in Christ which alone brought salvation, that he needed no intermediary between him and God, and that the Bible was the exclusive source of religious truth. He and other Reformers had launched on Europe a Protestant Reformation which many were disposed to embrace. The printing-press carried these notions, so subversive of established religious authority and

teaching, far, fast and wide. Some secular rulers were also tempted
to accept them so as to bring the Church and its possessions more
D.2 firmly under their control (D.2). Henry VIII, king of England
and Wales, was not thus disposed at first. But from 1527 onwards
he wished to have his marriage to Catherine of Aragon annulled,
partly for political and partly for personal reasons. Only the Pope
had the authority to do this and he refused. So Henry and his
ministers tried to force him to change his mind. Parliament passed
a number of Acts, as applicable to Wales as England, culminating
in the transfer of the Pope's authority to the King and making
D.3 Henry Supreme Head of the Church in England (D.3). This was
not a Protestant Reformation but it was the first decisive step
towards it. As far as Wales was concerned, unlike parts of
southern and eastern England, there was little or no sympathy for
Protestant doctrine. The central fact about the Reformation in
Wales was that it was not at first of the people's making. It was
imposed on them from above and from outside by authority of
King and Parliament. The government required laymen in
authority and all the clergy to take an oath of loyalty to Henry as
Supreme Head. In Wales, almost without exception, they did so
D.4 (D.4). Some were uneasy about the King's actions and there was
D.5 much sympathy for Queen Catherine (D.5). But only two
clergymen, neither of them Welsh, are known to have refused the
oath, though at least four Welsh clerics, living in England, were
executed for refusing it.

Henry and his chief advisor, *Thomas Cromwell*, proceeded to
exploit the financial potential of the supremacy by dissolving the
monasteries and transferring their assets to the Crown. Between
1536 and 1540 all forty-seven of the monasteries and friaries of
Wales were suppressed. They disappeared without any recorded
protest or opposition; not because they were dens of immorality
but because they seemed to have outlived their purpose. The
number of monks was too small to enable them to maintain a full
round of worship and prayer, with an average of only seven or
eight in larger houses like Neath or Conway and about three in
D.6 smaller ones like Monmouth or Beddgelert (D.6). Though some
monasteries maintained a measure of learning, hospitality and
poor relief, they were no longer making significant contributions
in these respects as once they had done. Nor were they the active

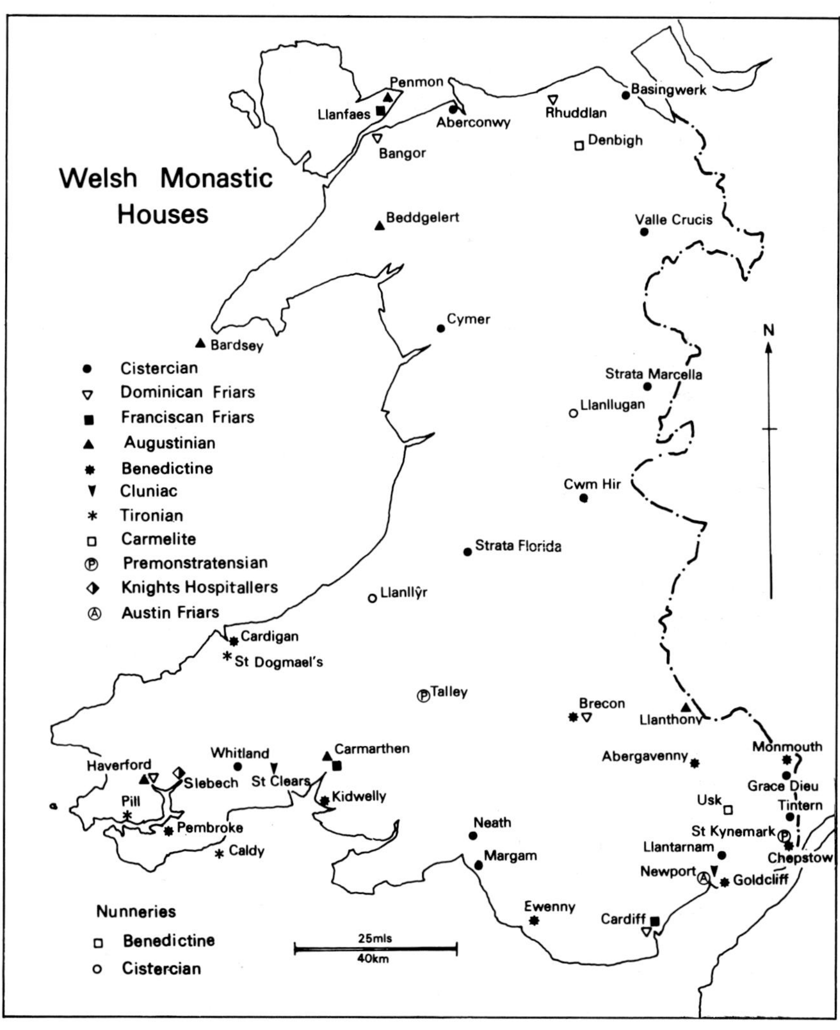

Welsh Monastic Houses
Cistercian
Dominican Friars
Franciscan Friars
Augustinian
Benedictine
Cluniac
Tironian
Carmelite
Premonstratensian
Knights Hospitallers
Austin Friars
Nunneries
Benedictine
Cistercian
25mls
40km
N
Penmon
Llanfaes
Aberconwy
Bangor
Rhuddlan
Basingwerk
Denbigh
Beddgelert
Valle Crucis
Bardsey
Cymer
Strata Marcella
Llanllugan
Cwm Hir
Strata Florida
Llanllŷr
Cardigan
St Dogmael's
Talley
Brecon
Llanthony
Monmouth
Abergavenny
Grace Dieu
Usk
Tintern
St Kynemark
Chepstow
Llantarnam
Newport
Goldcliff
Haverford
Whitland
Carmarthen
Slebech
St Clears
Kidwelly
Pill
Pembroke
Caldy
Neath
Margam
Ewenny
Cardiff

pioneers in economic initiative that they had been; they were now content to turn over the management of their estates and much else to laymen. When the monasteries were dissolved, some monks were pensioned off, others became parish priests and a few may have returned to lay life. Monastic buildings were pillaged of stone, metalwork and timber, and fell into ruin, though some monastic churches such as those of Chepstow and Haverfordwest, were allowed to remain as parish churches, while other buildings became houses for the gentry, like Ewenni or Margam. Great landmark though it was in the history of religion, the dissolution passed with curiously little upheaval. The monasteries had become so secularized and outmoded that they could be appropriated with little fear of the consequences. The leading gentry were only too eager to benefit from their disappearance and acquired their property sooner or later.

A cause of greater concern to the authorities than the *dissolution of the monasteries* was the possible reaction to the abolition in 1538 of shrines and centres of pilgrimage associated with the monasteries and the cathedrals. When the very popular centre of the cult of the Virgin Mary at Pen-rhys in the Rhondda was about to be broken up, instructions were given that it should be done at night as secretly as possible for fear of riot or disturbance. At St David's, Bishop William Barlow, the most ardent Protestant sent to Wales in Henry VIII's reign, met with stubborn hostility to his attacks on the shrine of St David and his proposals to move his
D.7 cathedral to Carmarthen (D.7). Yet even these measures against shrines aroused no open risings. The poet, Lewys Morgannwg, may have been expressing the sentiments of many when he praised the King for dealing with the Pope as firmly as his other enemies
D.8 (D.8). His subjects approved of Henry's strong, positive rule. Besides, his changes made little difference to everyday religious observance. The churches looked much the same as before; their services had hardly been altered; and Latin was still the language of worship. The King could almost have been said to have maintained popery without the Pope; and if he executed Welshman Edward Powell for upholding papal authority, he also burnt
D.9 Thomas Capper of Cardiff for Protestant heresy (D.9). During his reign the whole emphasis was on political cohesion not doctrinal innovation.

That could not be said of his son's reign. The boy-king, Edward VI (1547–53), was pushed by his advisors far and fast along the road to a Protestant state. There were three main trends of change. First, there were further raids on church property such as *chantries* and colleges, endowed to offer prayers for the dead, and church plant and ornaments were seized in the name of reform. Secondly, many long-cherished features of medieval religious practice were abolished; images, pictures and roodlofts were destroyed; saints' days and traditional ceremonies done away with; and altars thrown down and replaced by tables. Thirdly, and most significant, the Protestant and English First and Second Books of Common Prayer (1549 and 1552) were introduced at the expense of the Latin and Catholic service books. This created great difficulty in Wales, where most of the population did not understand English. All these changes were very badly received in Wales. They had been introduced at far too hectic a pace to a population which was largely unprepared for them and found them alien and unintelligible. Some of the poetry of the time reveals how bitterly they were
D.10 resented (D.10).

In some parts of the kingdom such alterations had led to serious rebellion. Some contemporary observers had predicted trouble in Wales, but none had come. Why not? The answer may perhaps lie in a combination of religious and secular factors. Those forces which had insulated the Welsh against Protestant heresy and criticism also tended to seal them off against the most powerful of *orthodox* reforming trends. The very absence of criticism or controversy was in itself a clear indication of an unsound condition of religion. It came about because most of the Welsh, lay and cleric alike, tended to be badly-instructed and superficial in their religious belief.

At the same time there were particularly powerful inducements encouraging the dominant class of landowning gentry to follow the lead given by a strong monarchy. The Crown could offer solid political and economic possibilities of advancement which, dovetailing into the family ambitions of the gentry, would be likely to work against the Church. It would have been remarkable if the gentry had turned their backs on a loyalty to the Tudors materially so rewarding and psychologically so

satisfying to them. Yet men are sometimes prepared to sacrifice self-interest and pledge their support to a higher loyalty. They might perhaps have done so now on behalf of the Church, had the clergy given them a clear lead in that direction. This the clergy seemed quite unable to do. The bishops and higher clergy were mostly civil servants, appointed as the result of the King's influence and unwilling to disobey him; the lower clergy were usually poor, ill-educated and often unaware of the issues at stake; and the life of the monks was inert and uninspired. The result was that the clergy collapsed abjectly before the inexorable pressure of the state. No doubt many men had profound misgivings about what the government was doing, especially during Edward VI's reign, when there were serious
D.11 fears of rebellion in Wales (D.11). Such was the supine quality of religion and belief, however, that these doubts did not seem to go very deep. Most men quietly stuck to their old ways, outwardly accepted the government's orders, inwardly kept their own counsel, and hoped that the changes would not last.

Not surprisingly, therefore, during the reign of Catholic Mary I (1553–1558), most of the Welsh were not loth to return in her wake to the familiar Roman fold. Some of the poets suggested that the people were glad to see the mass restored and
D.12 the altars set up anew (D.12). True, there was upheaval among the priesthood, a number of whom were deprived of their livings for marriage and a few for heresy. But there were
D.12a only three martyrs for heresy in the whole of Wales (D.12a), which gives an indication of how slight Protestant support was, though this should not be over-emphasized, since there was only one martyr in all the English counties west of Salisbury. Nor should it be thought that there was a simple turning back of the clock to 1529. Too much had happened in the meantime, and the gentry insisted upon keeping the gains they had made out of church property. Mary's marriage to Philip of Spain and her war with France were deeply disliked; and bad harvests and a devastating influenza epidemic added to the unpopularity of her regime. Even among the Welsh there was a handful of Protestant enthusiasts; mostly young Oxford graduates converted at university, or prominent figures in towns like Carmarthen. Most of them wisely kept their heads down during

Mary's reign, as did William Salesbury, while about half a dozen, including Richard Davies the future bishop, went into exile to Protestant cities on the Continent. Among the staunch Marian Catholics some of the best, like Thomas Goldwell, bishop of St Asaph, and Morus Clynnog and Gruffudd Robert, wanted to reinvigorate the Roman Church by introducing the ideals of
D.13 Catholic reform into Wales (D.13). In doing so they laid the foundations of subsequent Catholic opposition to Elizabeth I. Had Mary's reign lasted another ten or fifteen years they might have made Wales a devoutly Catholic country.

After Elizabeth succeeded Mary in November 1558, one of her first acts of policy in the spring of 1559 was to establish a cautious and moderate Anglican Church based on the Second Edwardian Prayer Book of 1552. As events turned out, this settlement ensured the success of the Reformation in England and Wales. It was received in Wales without opposition but without any enthusiasm either. Partly this came about out of respect for the Church 'by law established', partly because people were uncertain what the future might hold if Elizabeth married or died, partly out of bewilderment caused by previous rapid changes, partly from caution, and partly because their commitment to religion was not so intense as to impel men to put themselves at risk. Throughout Elizabeth's reign (1558–1603), there continued to be a good deal of indifference, uncertainty and uneasy compromise. The allegiance of the largely inert mass of the population was being fought for by two minorities — one Catholic, the other Protestant — both of them articulate, dedicated and determined. They had much in common. Both were sincerely patriotic and deeply influenced by Renaissance learning. Each was committed to using the Welsh language in an effort to raise the level of belief and purify worship and behaviour. The Catholics wanted to see Roman religion revived and cleansed of its excesses. Their opponents wished to introduce Reformed belief and worship based on the authority of the Scriptures. Neither, however, could ignore political considerations, which continued to exert a decisive influence. The leaders of the Welsh Catholic resistance, whether clerics like Gruffudd Robert or Owen Lewis, or lay conspirators such as Hugh Owen or Thomas Morgan, worked chiefly from Catholic

centres in Europe — Rome, Milan, Douai or Paris. They and their supporters in Wales depended on three main instruments in trying to bring about a Catholic reconversion. First there were the young men trained as priests in seminaries like those at Douai or Rome and smuggled back into the country to minister in secret. About a hundred were recruited in Wales, though only a small minority came back there to minister. Brave and utterly dedicated, they faced persecution and even death with great
D.14 courage (D.14). Secondly, the Catholics published books, manuscripts and poems, in Welsh and English, setting forth their faith and circulated them clandestinely among the faithful
D.15 (D.15). They even founded three short-lived presses in Wales. Thirdly, they participated in plots and conspiracies designed to assassinate Elizabeth, raise rebellions and organize foreign invasion. Though some Welshmen were implicated in such intrigues, they were not popular and tended to unleash a
D.16 powerful patriotic backlash in Wales (D.16). By the end of Elizabeth's reign there were only 808 *recusants* (open Catholic objectors) as compared with 212,450 regular churchgoers. The Counter-Reformation had failed; it had found its task of overcoming the Protestant government and establishment too formidable.

In spite of the advantages which Protestants enjoyed as upholders of the Church established by the Queen and having a virtual monopoly of access to press and pulpit, the two main channels for influencing public opinion, they had their difficulties too. Though thirteen out of sixteen bishops in Elizabethan Wales were Welsh, including two or three of outstanding ability, and most of them earnest Protestants and resident in their sees, many of their clergy were men of indifferent zeal and quality. Most Welsh parishes were too unremunerative to attract as their incumbents men who had been educated at grammar schools or university and from whose
D.17 ranks alone licensed preachers could be recruited (D.17). Poor livings, moreover, led to pluralism (holding more than one living at a time) and absenteeism. Only slowly could the Elizabethan Church hope to see the back of the inferior clergy it had inherited and try to recruit better successors to them. By the end of the reign, however, it had succeeded to some extent in

raising the general standard. The number of priests who had had higher education had markedly increased, and among the higher clergy were men of real distinction and commitment, like Edmwnd Prys or Edward James.

Nor was it only the clergy of whom the bishops and other
critics had cause to complain; the laity also came under their
censure. There were reports of widespread ignorance, superstition and the survival of Catholic practices at all social
D.18 levels (D.18). Many of the gentry were slack in executing their
duty to enforce the religious settlement and some had warm
D.19 Catholic sympathies (D.19). Others followed with alacrity the
lead given them by more than one Tudor administration in
plundering and exploiting the possessions and revenues of the
Church. In fairness to the laity, nevertheless, it should be
remembered that from their ranks emerged some of the most
active reformers and authors and their sponsors — men like
William Salesbury, Morus Kyffin and Humphrey Toy. This was
eloquent testimony to the Reformation's shift of emphasis to an
increased role in religious life for the learned and pious layman.
Furthermore, by 1603 many of the squires had come to view the
Established Church as one of the sturdiest bulwarks of political
and social order and stability, which was probably the decisive
factor in accounting for their support of it.

The most critical need of the Elizabethan Church, though,
was for a Welsh version of the Bible and the Book of Common
Prayer. The achievement of such a translation was its decisive
victory. An Act of Parliament of 1563 authorized the translation
and required its use in all parishes where Welsh was normally
D.20 spoken (D.20). The Welsh New Testament and Prayer Book,
largely the work of William Salesbury and Richard Davies,
appeared in 1567; William Morgan's complete Bible in 1588
D.21 (D.21). They were accompanied by the translation of the
catechism, the Book of Homilies, and other religious classics
into Welsh. The publication of this literature, though less in
volume than the Reformers had originally hoped for, ensured
the success of the Reformation in Wales. Without it, Protestant
teaching would have been a meaningless farce amid a monoglot
Welsh-speaking population. English services were no better
understood than the Latin had been in what *George Owen* had

D.22 called the 'time of blindness' (D.22). Making Welsh the language of public worship gave it enhanced status and ensured its survival. The Welsh Bible, combining the vigour and purity of the classical language of the *bards* with an extended flexibility and range, laid the foundation for all subsequent Welsh literature. It was accompanied by a dramatic historical re-interpretation which rejected emphatically the notion that the Reformation was a new-fangled heresy and an alien English creed. On the contrary, it was presented as a renaissance of the earliest British Church and a revival of the Golden
D.23 Age of the British forefathers of the Welsh (D.23). As such, it proved an immensely potent factor in preserving and stimulating Welsh patriotism.

At the end of the sixteenth century, however, life remained as hard, if not harder than ever for the still largely illiterate masses. It was still true to say that only a minority among Welsh clerics and laymen, nearly all drawn from the upper classes, understood and accepted wholeheartedly Reformation doctrines. But they were the decisive shapers of opinion, with an influence out of all proportion to their numbers. They would ensure that the future lay with a Protestant Wales.

## Sources

D.1 There is an image of Derfel Gadarn . . . in whom the people have so great confidence, hope and trust that they come daily on pilgrimage unto him; some with kine, and others with oxen or horses, and the rest with money; insomuch that there were 500 or 600 pilgrims to a man's estimation that offered to the said image the fifth day of this present month of April. The innocent people hath been sore allured and enticed to worship the said image, insomuch that there is a common saying amongst them that whosoever will offer anything to the said image of Derfel Gadarn, he hath power to fetch him or them that so offer out of Hell when they be damned.

(Ellis Price to Thomas Cromwell, April 1538. Thos. Wright, *The Suppression of the Monasteries*, 1843, pp.190–1).

D.2 A phan roes [y brenin] eisoes gymaint o ddoniau presennol i genedl y Cymry ni fydd llesgach i ganiatau iddynt ddoniau ysbrydol.

Am hynny gweddus yw rhoi yn Gymraig beth o'r Ysgrythur lan, o herwydd bod llawer o Gymry a fedr ddarllen Cymraeg heb fedru darllen un gair o Saesneg na Lladin, ac yn enwedig y pynciau sy'n angenrheidiol i bob rhyw Gristion eu gwybod dan berygl ei enaid, sef yw hynny: pynciau'r ffydd Gatholig, a'r weddi a ddysgodd Duw inni, a elwir y Pader, a'r Deng Ngair Deddf . . .

Ac er bod y rhain gyda llawer o bethau da eraill yn ysgrifenedig mewn bagad o hen lyfrau Cymraeg, eto nid yw'r llyfrau hynny'n gyffredinol ymysg y bobl. Ac yn awr y rhoes Duw y print yn ein mysg ni er amlhau gwybodaeth ei eirau bendigedig ef, iawn yw i ni, fel y gwnaeth holl Gristnogaeth heb law, gymryd rhan o'r daioni hwnnw gyda hwy fel na bai ddiffrwyth rhodd cystal a hon i ni mwy nag i eraill . . .

Ac am hynny gyda gweled fod rhan fawr o'm cenedl y Cymry mewn tywyllwch afrifed o eisiau gwybodaeth Duw a'i orchmynion ac oherwydd hynny y digwyddant mewn dyfnder pechodau . . .

(And since [the King] has already given so many temporal gifts to the Welsh nation he will be no more loth to allow them spiritual gifts.

Therefore it is fitting to translate into Welsh some of the Holy Scriptures since there are many Welsh people who can read Welsh, though they cannot read a single word of English or Latin, especially those matters which every Christian should know at the peril of his soul: namely the chief items of the Creed, the Lord's Prayer and the Ten Commandments . . .

And although these things, together with many other good things, are found in writing in many old Welsh manuscripts, yet these manuscripts are not common among the people. And now that God has given us the printing-press in our midst to multiply knowledge of his blessed words, it is right for us, as all Christendom has done besides, to take a share in that virtue with them, so that a gift as excellent as this should not be without fruit for us as for others . . .

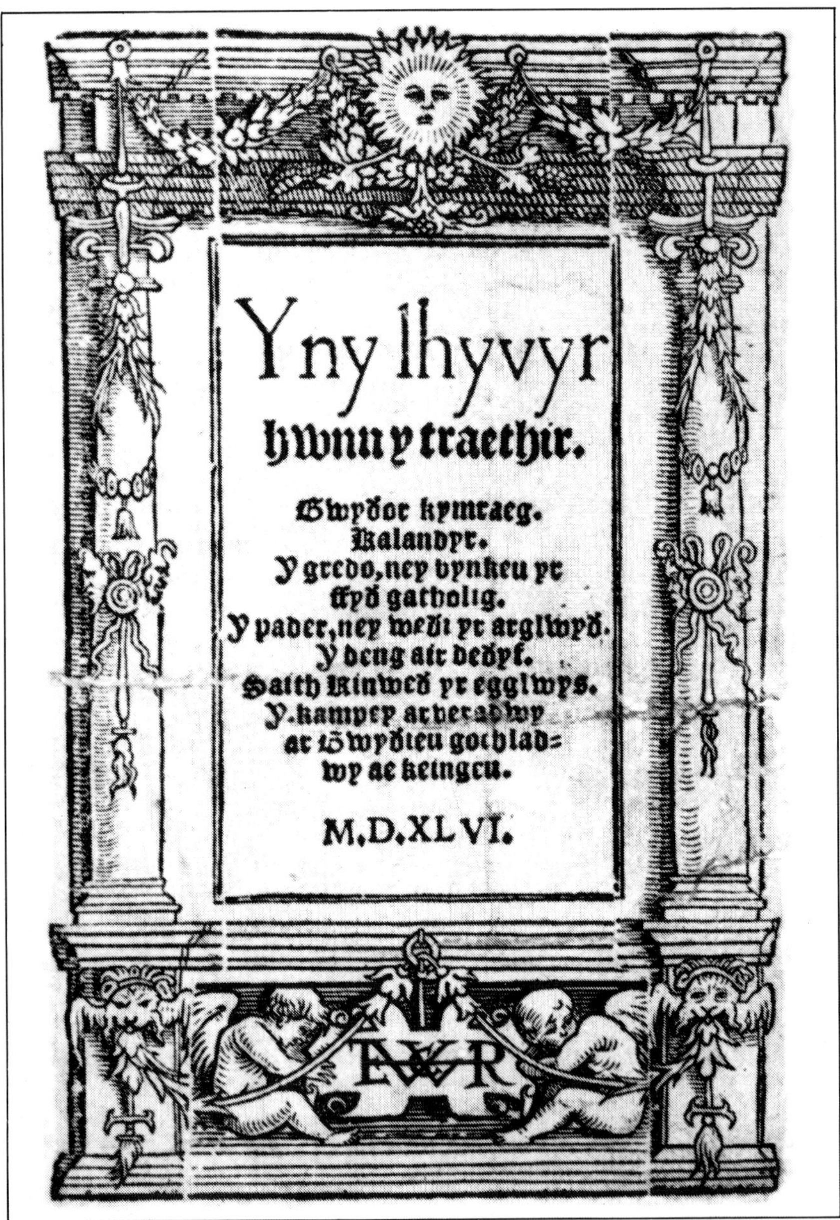

Yny lhyvyr
hwnn y traethir.

Gwyðor kymraeg.
Kalandyr.
Y gredo, ney bynkeu yr
ffyð gatholig.
Y pader, ney weði yr arglwyð.
Y deng air deðyf.
Saith Rinweð yr egglwys.
Y kampeu arveradwy
ar Gwyðieu gochlad=
wy ar keingeu.

M.D.XLVI.

The Title page of *Yny Lhyvyr Hwnn* . . . (*Source: National Library of Wales.*)

For that reason, because I see that a large part of my nation the Welsh is lost in untold darkness for want of knowledge of God's words and his commandments and for that reason falls into the depths of sin.)

(Sir John Price, *Yny lhyvyr Hwnn* . . . G.H. Hughes, *Rhagymadroddion, 1547–1659*, 1951, pp.3–4).

D.3 Be it enacted by authority of the present Parliament that the King . . . shall be taken, accepted and reputed the only Supreme Head in earth of the Church of England called *Anglicana Ecclesia*, and shall have and enjoy annexed and united to the imperial crown of this realm as well as the title and style thereof, as all the honours etc. . . . to the said dignity of Supreme Head of the same Church belonging and appertaining.

(Act of Supremacy, 1534. G.R. Elton, *The Tudor Constitution*, 1982, p.355).

D.4 We, the Prior and Convent of Ewenny, in the diocese of Llandaff, with one mouth and one voice, and by the unanimous consent of all, by this our writing, given under our common seal, in our Chapter-house on behalf of ourselves and our successors, each and all will always pay entire, inviolate, sincere and perpetual fidelity, observance, and obedience to our Lord, King Henry the Eighth, and to Anne, his wife, and to his offspring lawfully begotten . . . and that we will notify and preach the same things to the people wherever time and occasion shall be granted. Also that we hold it confirmed and ratified for ever, and will hold it in perpetuity, that our aforesaid King Henry is Head of the English Church. Also that the Bishop of Rome, who in his Bulls usurps the name of Pope and arrogates to himself the supreme Pontificate, has no other jurisdiction conferred upon him by God in this kingdom of England than any other foreign bishop.

(Oath taken by the Prior and two monks on 11 September 1534. J.P. Turbervill, *Ewenny Priory*, 1901, p.49).

D.5 As to the indisposition of the people of Wales . . . I understand they are very angry at the treatment of the Queen [Catherine] and

Princess [Mary] and also at what is done against the faith, for they have always been good Christians . . . and it is said that the people only wait for a chief to take the field.

(Chapuys, the imperial ambassador, to Charles V, 3 November 1534. *Letters and Papers of Henry VII's Reign*, vol.vii, 1863).

D.6 . . . there was no pot, nor pan, nor monk in the said house [Monmouth] except one who boards in the town. The prior is in sanctuary at Garwey. It is of the King's foundation and all the country marvels that there is no reformation, as it can spend 60 pounds a year all charges borne . . . I intend to suppress the said house for the voice of the country is that while ye have monks there ye shall have neither good rule nor good order there; and I hear such saying by the common people of all the houses of monks that ye have within Wales.

(John Vaughan, monastic visitor, to Thomas Cromwell, 1536. G. Williams, *The Welsh Church from Conquest to Reformation*, 1962, p.389).

D.7 I admonished the canons of St David's . . . in no wise to set forth feigned relics for to allure the people to superstition . . . On St David's Day, the people wilfully solemnizing the feast, certain relics were set forth which I caused to be sequestered . . . Furthermore, though I might seem more presumptuous than needeth to motion any suit for the translation of the see from St David's to Carmarthen . . . I might there settle my continual consistory, assisted with learned persons, maintaining a free grammar school, with a daily lecture of Holy Scripture, whereby God's honour preferred, the Welsh rudeness decreasing, Christian civility may be introduced to the famous renown of the King's supremacy.

(William Barlow to Thomas Cromwell, March 1538. Wright, *Suppression of the Monasteries*, 1843, pp.184–5).

D.8 Amhauwyr Duw ffydd mawr y diffoddaist
. . . anghredwyr Iesu tan a gynneuaist
Y mer a'u holl esgyrn meirw y llosgaist . . .

Ddoe Esgob Rhufain o ddysg y profaist,
Y sy i'th deyrnas o'i waith a ddernaist;
I'n dallu elyn ei dwyll a welaist,
Am aur dy ynys yma yr ordeiniaist,
Y sel a'i gyfraith hyn a ddiffeithaist,
Yn iach mwy hynny, yn wych ymwahenaist.
Ffalswyr crefyddwyr a'u cor a feiddaist
Am dwyll a phechod i'r llawr y'u dodaist.

(The doubters of God's great faith thou hast destroyed . . . those who did not believe in Jesus thou hast consigned to the flames and burnt their dead bones to the marrow . . . Thou hast tried yesterday the Bishop of Rome by thy learning and shattered what remained of his work within thy kingdom; thou has shown how the enmity of his deceit blinded us; thou has ordained that the gold of the island shall remain here; his seal and his law thou hast destroyed. Farewell to all that; well hast thou done to part us from it. The false monks and their chancels thou hast overthrown and their fraud and sin hast cast to the ground.)

(Lewys Morgannwg to Henry VIII, Williams, *Welsh Church*, 1962, p.546).

D.9 Out of which there is allowed to them [the bailiffs of Cardiff] 4s.4d. for costs and expenses sustained in burning Thomas Capper, who was attainted of heresy at Cardiff . . . being in prison there by the space of 130 days.

(Bailiffs' Accounts, 1542-43. *Cardiff Records*, vol.I, 1898, p.225).

D.10

Nyni droeson gan ffydd Sayson,
Ni ddaw ein calonnau ni byth yn eu lle . . .
Fe aeth dy demlau yma a thraw
Oll yn llaw y lleygion;
A'th eglwysi ymhob lle
Yn gornelau gweigion . . .
Briwio'r allorau mawr eu braint
A'u troi yn ddifraint ddigon;
Gosod trestel yn ddiglod
Fel gwarchiod gweddwon;
Wedi ysbeilio Duw a'i dy . . .

(We have been turned by the faith of the English, our hearts will never return to their rightful place . . . Thy temples have, hither and thither, all gone into the hands of laymen; and thy churches everywhere are nothing but empty corners . . . Destroying the altars once so privileged and turning them into deprived objects; placing an unhonoured testle like a widow's boards; having despoiled God and his house . . . )

(Tomas ab Ieuan ap Rhys, *Hen Gwndidau*, in L.H. James and T.C. Evans, (eds.), *Hen Gwndidau, Carolau a chywyddau*, 1910, pp.33, 39, 44).

D.11 He saith that in the time of rebellion in Devonshire and Cornwall threatening to come into Wales, he, teaching the people the true form of prayer according to God's holy word and declaring the prayer upon beads to be vain and superstitious, yet dared not, for fear of tumult, forcibly take from any man his beads without authority.

(Robert Ferrar, bishop of St David's, referring to events of 1549. John Foxe, *Acts and Monuments*, ed. Cattley and Townshend, (eds.), vol.VII, 1837–41, p.13).

D.12

Wele fraint y saint yn neshau — eilwaith
Wele'r hen 'fferennau'
Wele Dduw a'i law ddehau
Yn gallu oll ein gwellhau.

(Behold once more the privilege of the saints draws near, behold the old masses; behold God making us whole with his right hand.)

(Sion Brwynog, 1553. W. Ambrose Bebb, *Cyfnod y Tuduriaid*, 1939, p.93).

D.12a Now when he perceived that his time was no less near than it was reported unto him, he sent forthwith to his wife and willed her by the messenger that in any wise she would make ready and send unto him his wedding garment, meaning a shirt, which afterwards he was burned in . . . Thus dies this godly and old man, Rawlins [White] for the testimony of God's truth.

(Foxe's account of the burning of Rawlins White, 1555, *Acts and Monuments*, vol.VII, 1837–41, pp.32–3).

D.13 That no priest do from henceforth haunt, resort or repair to any diceing houses or common bowling alleys, or any other suspect houses or places, or otherwise behave themselves unjustly or unseemly, upon pain of deprivation of their benefices.

(Injunctions of Bishop Goldwell of St Asaph, 1556. D.R. Thomas, *History of the Diocese of St Asaph*, vol.I, 1908, p.87).

D.14 In the primitive church, when there were more pagans than Christians, rather than they would deny their faith, they yielded to any kind of death . . . Even so, I submit myself to any death whatsoever before I will forsake the Catholic faith.

(Edward Jones, seminary priest, martyred May 1590. T.P. Ellis, *Welsh Catholic Martyrs*, 1933, p.48).

D.15 . . . yr awrhon myfi a glywaf fod aml leoedd yng Nghymru, ie, siroedd cyfan heb un Cristion ynddynt, yn byw fel anifeiliaid, y rhan fwyaf ohonynt heb wybod dim oddi wrth ddaioni, ond eu bod yn dal enw Crist yn eu cof, heb wybod haeachen beth yw Crist mwy nag anifeiliaid. A'r mannau lle y mae rhai ohonynt yn Gristnogion, nid oes ond rhai tlodion cyffredin yn canlyn Crist. Mae'r boneddigion a'r rhai cyfoethog heb feddwl am ffydd yn y byd heb fod na thwymyn nac oer.

(. . . and now I hear that there are many places in Wales, yea, whole shires knowing nothing of virtue, except that they retain the name of Christ in their memory, knowing hardly anything more of what Christ is than animals do. And in those places where some of them are Christians, only a few poor common people follow Christ. The gentry and the wealthy think nothing of any faith in the world and are neither hot nor cold.)

(Anon. *Drych Cristianogawl*, 1585. Hughes, *Rhagymadroddion*, 1951, p.52).

D.16 I protest I would sooner spend my living and my life also than that the enemy should possess any of Her Majesty's dominions.

(Sir John Wogan, 1599. G. Williams, *Welsh Reformation Essays*, 1967, p.27).

D.17 . . . I most humbly beseech your Lordships of your Christian care to God's religion and service and for furtherance of the Queen's Majesty's most godly zeal to become protectors and defenders of the Church in my diocese that it be no further troubled, spoiled or impoverished. But that small patrimony of the Church which is yet remaining to the maintenance of God's service, may so still continue to the sustentation (as I trust) of preachers and teachers, after that the incumbents now being no preachers shall happen to depart.

(Report on his diocese of St David's by Bishop Richard Davies, January 1570. D.R. Thomas, *Life and Work of Bishop Davies and William Salesbury*, 1902, p.44).

D.18 . . . Ignorance continueth many in the dregs of superstition . . . images and altars standing in the churches undefaced, lewd and indecent vigils and watches observed, much pilgrimage-going, many candles set up to the honour of the saints, some relics yet carried about, and all the country full of beads and knots.

(Report on the diocese of Bangor by Bishop Nicholas Robinson, 1567. David Mathew, 'Some Elizabethan Documents', *Bulletin of the Board of Celtic Studies*, VI, 1933, 77–8).

. . . I perceive a great number to be slow and cold in the true service of God; some careless for any religion; and some that wish the romish religion again.

(Davies's report, 1570. Thomas, *Davies and Salesbury*, op.cit., p.38).

Hence flow our swarms of soothsayers and enchanters, such as will not stick openly to profess that they walk on Tuesdays and Thursdays at nights with the fairies, of whom they brag

Bishop William Morgan. (*Source: National Library of Wales.*)

themselves to have their knowledge. . . . Hence proceed open defending of Purgatory and the Real Presence, praying unto images etc., with other infinite monsters.

(John Penry, *The Aequity of an Humble Supplication* (1587). Ed. David Williams, *Three Treatises*, 1960, p.33).

D.19 They [the magistrates] apply their power to further and continue the kingdom of Antichrist. They defend papistry, superstition and idolatry, pilgrimages to wells and blind chapels, and they procure the wardens of churches in time of visitation to perjury, to conceal images, roodlofts and altars. Here would I wish that the justices of the peace with us in Wales should receive admonition and learning, although I speak generally of them, yet I know that some of them walk uprightly and more after the will of God than others do.

(Richard Davies, *Funeral Sermon . . . for the Earl of Essex*, 1577 in Thomas, *Davies and Salesbury*, op.cit., p.49).

D.20 That the Bishops of Hereford, St David's, Asaph, Bangor and Llandaff and their Successors shall take such order amongst themselves for the Souls' health of the flocks committed to their charge within Wales, that the whole Bible, containing the New Testament and the Old, with the Book of Common Prayer and Administration of the Sacraments, as is now used within this realm in English, to be truly and exactly translated into the British or Welsh tongue.

(Act for the Translation of the Bible, 1563. Ivor Bowen, *The Statutes of Wales*, 1908, p.150).

D.21 For although it is much to be desired that the inhabitants of the same island should be of the same speech and tongue, yet it is to be equally considered that to attain this end so much time and trouble are required that in the meantime God's people would be suffered to perish from the hunger of his word, which would be barbarous and cruel beyond measure. Further there can be no doubt that similarity and agreement in religion rather than in speech much more promotes unity. To prefer unity to piety,

Y BEIBL CYS-
SEGR-LAN. SEF
YR HEN DESTA-
MENT, A'R NEWYDD.

2. Timoth. 3. 14, 15.

Eithr aros di yn y pethau a ddyſcaiſt, ac a ymddyried-
wyd i ti, gan wybod gan bwy y dyſcaiſt.
Ac i ti er yn fachgen wybod yr ſcrythur lân, yr hon
ſydd abl i'th wneuthur yn ddoeth i iechydwria-
eth, trwy'r ffydd yr hon ſydd yng-Hriſt Ieſu.

Imprinted at London by the Deputies of
CHRISTOPHER BARKER,
Printer to the Queenes moſt excel-
lent Maieſtie.

1588.

The title page of the Bible, 1588. (*Source: National Library of Wales.*)

expediency to religion, and a certain external concord among men to that extraordinary peace which the word of God impresses on the souls of men shows but little piety.

(William Morgan, Dedication to the Welsh Bible, 1588. A.O. Evans, *Memorandum on the Legality of the Welsh Bible*, 1925, p.134).

D.22 . . . (and now not three years past), we have had the light of the gospel, yea the whole Bible, in our native tongue, which in short time must needs work great good inwardly in the hearts of the people, whereas the service and the sacraments in the English tongue was as strange to many or most of the simplest sort as the mass in the time of blindness was to the rest of England.

(George Owen, *Dialogue of the Government of Wales* in Owen, *Penbrokeshire*, vol.III, 1892, p.57).

D.23 Felly, yr un modd y rhai y sy'n ddyfal ymdreiglo yn yr Ysgrythur lan sy yn dywedyd hwythau mai gorau ffydd yw'r ffydd hen, sef yr un y proffwydodd y proffwydi ohoni, yr hon a ddysgodd Crist a'i Apostolion i'r bobl yn eu hamser, a'r hon wedyn a gadarnhaodd y Merthyron a'u gwaed, gan dystio gyda hi a dioddef pob artaith hyd angau. Ac am hynny gwae'r neb a eilw hon yn newydd, o ba fodd bynnag y gwnel, ai o anwybod ai trwy wybod, i'w dwyllo'i hun ac i hudo'r bobl. At y ffydd hon yn ei Epistol yma uchod y mae'r anrhydeddus Dad, R.D., ail Dewi Mynyw, yn ceisio'ch gwahodd, eich llwybro a'ch arwain oll am yr enaid.

(So, in the same way those who are deeply learned in Holy Scriptures also say that the best faith is the old faith, namely the one of which the prophets prophesied, the one which Christ and his Apostles taught the people in their time, and the one which the Martyrs later confirmed with their blood, sealing their testimony to it with every torture even to death. And for that reason, woe unto him who calls this new, whysoever he does so, whether from ignorance or consciously to deceive himself and to seduce the people. It is to this faith, in his Epistle above, that the honourable Father, Richard Davies, second Dewi of St David's, seeks to invite, direct and lead you all for your souls' sake.)

(William Salesbury, Introduction to the New Testament, 1567. Hughes, *Rhagymadroddion*, 1951, p.44).

## Debating the Evidence

The revolutionary religious changes of the Tudor period were put into effect by Acts of Parliament. Two of the most crucial are quoted here. The Act of Supremacy fractured a thousand years of history as the monarch replaced the Pope as head of the church in England, so transforming the Welsh church too. In Elizabeth's reign an act was passed which had immense significance for the religious, educational and linguistic history of Wales, the Act for the Translation of the Bible into Welsh.

Much of the other evidence used here is literary — letters, appeals, forewords to religious writings and three examples of that corpus of difficult source material, poetry.

*Source D.1*

*Thomas Cromwell* was Henry VIII's chief minister in 1538 and the man most responsible for implementing Reformation changes. How might this information affect your perception of this document? Is it possible to reach a fair assessment of the nature of popular belief and devotion from a source such as this? What does it tell us about people's religious priorities and habits?

*Source D.2*

This is an extract from a book published in 1546/1547 and was the first to be printed in Welsh. What does this tell you of the author? What counterpoint between religious teaching, printing and royal authority is woven in this passage? Does this relationship help to explain the success of the Reformation in Wales?

*Source D.3*

What are the significant phrases in this passage? What do words like 'imperial crown' and 'supreme head' tells us about the ideology of authority implied in the Statute?

*Source D.4*

In the light of what you know of the history of sixteenth-century religion and Reformation changes, is there anything in this document which indicates that interpretation of it might be difficult? Would you regard this as a 'forced' submission? What does the obedience-test imposed on the monks tell us about the priorities of the Reformation in England and Wales?

*Source D.5/D.6*
Should historians always bear in mind at whom statements are directed and for what purpose before using them as historical evidence?

*Source D.5*
Charles V was the Holy Roman Emperor. He was also a nephew of Catherine of Aragon, referred to in the document, the annulment of whose marriage to Henry VIII was the occasion of the Reformation crisis. Chapuys, as the acknowledgement states, was Charles's ambassador in England. How does this affect your interpretation of the document?

*Source D.6*
How far do statements such as this shape public opinion — rather than being shaped by it? Should we therefore dismiss them altogether?

*Source D.7*
What insight does the passage provide into pre-Reformation popular religion and into the priorities — administrative, educational, civilizing, as well as religious — of a reforming bishop?

*Source D.8*
What view does the passage convey of the nature of the Reformation as seen by Lewys Morgannwg? In what circumstances might poetry be a particularly useful historical source for our understanding of religious observance and belief?

*Source D.10*
What information about Tomas ab Ieuan ap Rhys would be essential before evaluating the worth of this source as historical evidence for Welsh people's attitudes to Reformation changes? What does the poet regard as the adverse effects of the Reformation?

*Source D.11, D.12*
In what way does the evidence in these sources help us to penetrate into popular attitudes towards the Reformation?

*Source D.11*
Why does it seem likely that Ferrar's evidence here is true?

*Sources D.12 and D.14*
Which of these documents is the better historical evidence?

*Source D.12a*
Were martyrs as essential to reformed religion as saints had been to pre-Reformation religion? Why do you think Foxe's *Acts and Monuments* became one of the most important, popular and influential books in England and Wales from the sixteenth century until the nineteenth century?

*Source D.15*
Is it possible to determine whether this passage was written by a protestant zealot or a Catholic exile? Does the fact that this document is anonymous make any difference to the historian's use of it?

*Source D.16*
How far would knowledge of Sir John Wogan's religious affiliations affect our assessment of the significance of this source?

*Sources D.17, D.18 and D.19*
To what extent, and in what ways, do these sources corroborate each other?

*Source D.17*
Why were the bishops so concerned with education and preaching?

*Source D.18*
How far are the religious shortcomings condemned in these passages coloured by the viewpoints of the observer? Do they help us to penetrate into the beliefs and practices of ordinary people in Elizabeth's reign?

*Source D.19*
How does Bishop Richard Davies conceive of the relationship between civilian government and religious orthodoxy?

*Source D.20*
What does this document tell us about the attitude of the government to the Welsh language? How far should our assessment be modified by Documents D.21 and D.22? Do these passages help us to understand

why Elizabeth's government sponsored the translation of the Bible into Welsh in spite of the general Tudor commitment to the virtues of linguistic uniformity?

*Source D.23*
Why were men of the early modern period so anxious to ground the validity of their innovations (as we see them) in the authority of a distant past?

## Discussion

How do we assess the strength of religious belief in Wales today? We can, of course, count the numbers of chapels open — and the ones which are derelict. Does that give us an answer? We can count the number of people who attend services. Do we choose Easter Sunday or mid- July for our count? We can ask people why they attend. Surely that would give us all the information we needed. Or would it? Assessing the strength of religious commitment in our own communities with a mass of documentation and oral evidence available is fraught with difficulties.

How much more so is assessment of religious affiliation and commitment in Tudor times. It is extremely difficult to empathize with the Roman Catholic monks of a Cistercian Abbey in mid Wales, for example, or to put ourselves in the position of an illiterate labourer reacting to the disappearance of images and wall paintings in the nearby Church (D.1). We can, of course, be certain that some religious leaders of both the Roman Catholic and the Protestant churches felt that these changes were a matter of life and death, in this world and the next. We have seen from the documents that there were martyrs on both sides (D.9, D.12a). When people were so committed that some felt sufficiently strongly to give their own lives for a cause we marvel at their bravery, but we do not expect them to be the most reliable of witnesses. We know what the State decreed; we have the Acts of Parliament such as the Act of Supremacy, to provide us with that information. What is far more difficult is to assess the impact of Reformation changes and the subsequent swings of the religious pendulum in the reigns of Edward VI, Mary I and Elizabeth I, especially among the mass of the unlettered population. When Ellis Price writes to *Thomas Cromwell* (D.1) to inform him of the popularity of the image of Derfel Gadarn is this an indication of deep-seated religious conviction on the part of the hundreds of pilgrims or is it merely a record of superstitious habit? Indeed, is there some reason why Ellis Price might be exaggerating? In the records in this section, more perhaps than in any other, we need to look carefully for evidence of exaggeration, bias and straightforward misrepresentation. The latter is highlighted in D.4. It is hardly to be expected that the inmates of Ewenny Priory experienced a sudden conversion. It could be that their commitment to their order and their faith was so lacking that they were prepared to acknowledge any change in the church, but save for denying Christ himself, they could hardly have done anything more sinful in the sight of their church than denying the headship of the Pope.

When we look at other evidence on the monastic orders it tends to reveal either a lack of idealism, or the martyr's courage, but not that the inmates of Ewenny, and their like, changed to solid conviction that they had been spiritually misguided over the centuries. The obvious explanation is that they wished to save their priory and themselves from an unknown fate. They were the victims of power politics who signed away their convictions from fear. Of course, that they were *not* prepared for the martyrdom which befell some later Roman Catholics *does* tell us something about the nature and the depth of their conviction, and that in turn highlights the reasons why Henry's radical changes met with relatively little dangerous opposition.

The potential to mislead of documents written from religious conviction is particularly marked. D.6 is typical of reports of agents who wrote what their master *Thomas Cromwell* wanted to receive. William Barlow (D.7) was an extreme Protestant for his time and viewed Roman practices in his diocese from that point of view. He is not so extreme, by far, as the next witness, Lewys Morgannwg. Poetry in any age is not expected to be neutral. This poem, D.8, is a polemic in favour of Henry VIII's religious changes, not surprisingly given the fact that it is a poetic tribute to the monarch. What purpose can such biased evidence serve, apart from telling us something of the nature of the *bardic* craft and patronage in Tudor Wales? It is not ideal evidence, of course, but medieval and Tudor *bardic* poetry picks up many of the nuances of anti-clericalism and popular response to religious changes which would otherwise be denied us. Looked at even more critically, with an even more questioning eye than most historical sources, the *bards* can tell us much about popular belief in Tudor Wales.

# *Government and Politics*

PENRY WILLIAMS

Did Tudor policy destroy the culture of Wales or introduce law and order into a misgoverned region? The question has been warmly debated for many years and will probably never be resolved to the satisfaction of all historians, for much depends upon subjective assessment. It is essential to distinguish between those matters that are firmly established and others that remain a matter of personal judgement. Both are part of history, and both will be presented here.

At the beginning of the sixteenth century Wales was divided between the shires of the Principality in the west and north-west, administered on a pattern similar to English counties, and the Marcher lordships of south and east Wales, which were to a great extent independent of the Crown. To establish some general control over the whole region the Crown had established the *Council in the Marches* during the reign of Edward IV; and this supervisory judicial body received greater authority from Wolsey in 1526. Relations between the Crown and the principal Marcher lords were governed by agreements, known as 'indentures', under which the lords were bound to administer justice effectively and to hand back criminals who fled from one lordship to another. Thanks to the *morcellation* of the region into dozens of independent jurisdictions, exercised often by self-interested lords and officers, complaints inevitably multiplied against the corruption of marcher officials, the maintenance of criminals by lords and
E.1 their servants, and the pervading lack of justice (E.1).

The response of the government was to appoint a strong-arm man, Bishop Rowland Lee, as President of the *Council in the Marches* in 1534. Lee revealed his outlook and his methods in a

E.2 letter to *Cromwell* describing how he dealt with outlaws (E.2).
Shortly after Lee's arrival in *the Marches* a series of statutes was
enacted in Parliament for tightening the administration of justice
in Wales. The most important of these (26 Henry VIII c.6)
regulated the conduct of Marcher courts, empowered English
judges to try various offences committed within the lordships, and
ordered criminals who had fled from one lordship to another to be
E.3 handed over to the *Council in the Marches* (E.3). But almost as it was
being enacted this policy was undermined by radical measures.
Proposals had already been made early in the decade for dividing
the Marcher lordships into shires on the English pattern; but these
had been shelved. In 1536 they were revived at the same time as
*Thomas Cromwell* began to assert the Crown's authority over
E.4 independent franchises in other parts of the realm (E.4). In this
parliamentary session were carried a statute for appointing
Justices of the Peace in the Welsh shires (27 Henry VIII c.5) and,
of even greater importance, the first 'act of union', entitled 'An
Act for Laws and Justice to be Ministered in Wales in like Form as
it is in this Realm' (27 Henry VIII c.26). The preamble emphasized
that although Wales had always been part of the realm, subject to
royal power, its different laws and language had produced discord
E.5 (E.5). The Marcher lordships were to be divided into shires,
seven new counties (Denbigh, Montgomery, Radnor, Brecknock,
Pembroke, Glamorgan and Monmouth) being added to the
existing six counties of the Principality. English laws were to be
E.6 enforced and English was to be the language of the courts (E.6).
Commissions were appointed to divide the counties into *hundreds*
and to enquire into the laws and customs of Wales. MPs were to be
chosen; one knight and one *burgess* for each shire.

This first statute laid down the lines for the changed structure
of government, but was in many respects imprecise. Its imple-
mentation was slow and tentative. Bishop Lee was strongly
opposed to the new policy, especially to the introduction of
E.7 Justices of the Peace (JPs) (E.7). The process of shiring was for a
time suspended and in 1540/1 a new set of proposals was put
forward for abolishing the *Council in the Marches* and erecting a
central *Chancery for Wales* together with a new Principality for
Prince Edward. But none of these proposals was adopted. Local
pressures from some of the gentry of Wales eventually ensured the

passage of the second 'act of union' in 1543. Mainly it built upon the foundation of the first, but the new statute was methodical and precise about the details of government, where the first had been vague. The apparatus of English county government was introduced into all the shires of Wales: sheriffs, JPs, coroners and constables. The *Council in the Marches* remained as the supervisory agency for the region, and common-law jurisdiction was en-
E.8 trusted to the four circuits of the *Courts of Great Sessions* (E.8).
E.9 English law was to govern the inheritance of land (E.9).

The significance of the 'acts of union' is not easily assessed. They have been seen as a measure of Welsh liberation and as agents for the destruction of Welsh culture. Probably they were neither. Wales had long been moving nearer to England in its laws and its culture, so that the 'union' came as the culmination of a process rather than a revolution; but some of the Welsh law and much of Welsh culture remained for many decades thereafter. The principal motives behind the acts are probably to be found in the desire of *Thomas Cromwell* for a more effective and uniform system of government, coupled with the anxiety of many Welsh gentry to be free from the jurisdiction of Marcher lords, rather than in ideological notions of national liberation or cultural suppression. Nor did the acts of 1536 and 1543 produce a union similar to the Scottish and Irish acts of 1707 and 1800, when national parliaments authorized incorporation into the larger realm. Wales was already part of the Tudor kingdom and the 'union' was as much a combination of its own *morcellated* fragments into a larger whole as it was a merger with England. Furthermore, the Henrician statutes and the establishment of the *Council in the Marches* were made possible only by the absorption into Crown hands of the most important lordships between 1461 and 1521. During the *Wars of the Roses* the Crown acquired by inheritance or forfeiture the Yorkist lordships of Denbigh, Builth and *the March*, as well as the Neville lordships of Glamorgan and Abergavenny. Henry Tudor's victory at *Bosworth* brought into Crown hands his family lordships in the south-west. Finally, the execution of the Duke of Buckingham in 1521 transferred the Stafford lordship of Brecknock to the King. By that date the King, as Marcher lord, had acquired control of all the great autonomous *fiefs* in the region. Only when that political supremacy had been

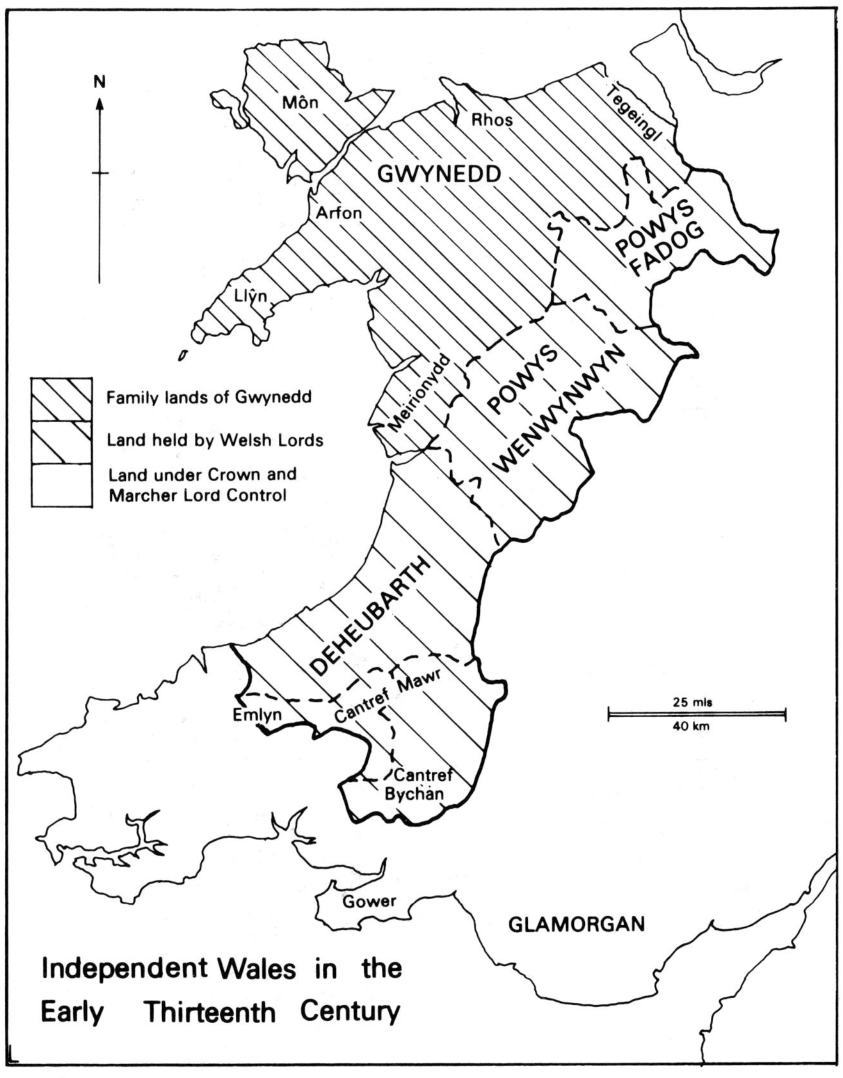


Independent Wales in the Early Thirteenth Century

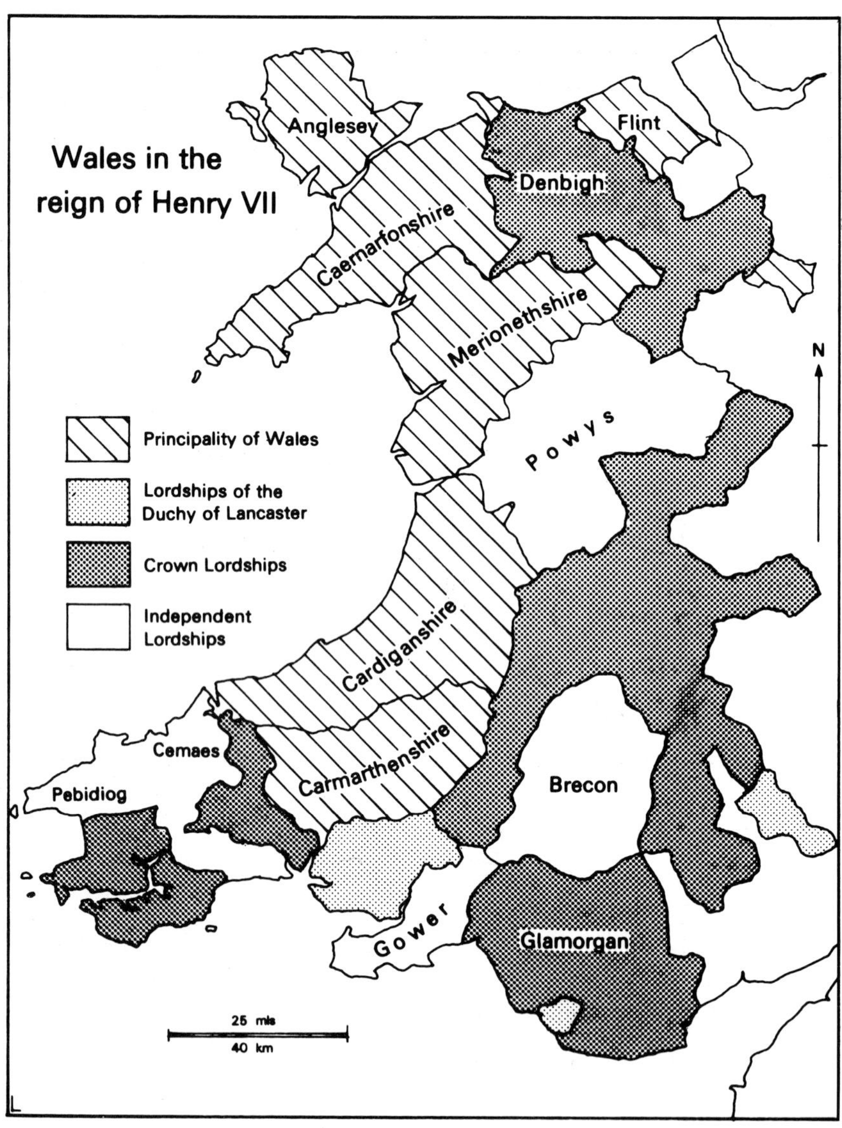
Wales in the
reign of Henry VII
Anglesey
Flint
Denbigh
Caernarfonshire
Merionethshire
Powys
Principality of Wales
Lordships of the
Duchy of Lancaster
Crown Lordships
Independent
Lordships
Cardiganshire
Carmarthenshire
Cemaes
Pebidiog
Brecon
Gower
Glamorgan
N
25 mls
40 km
L

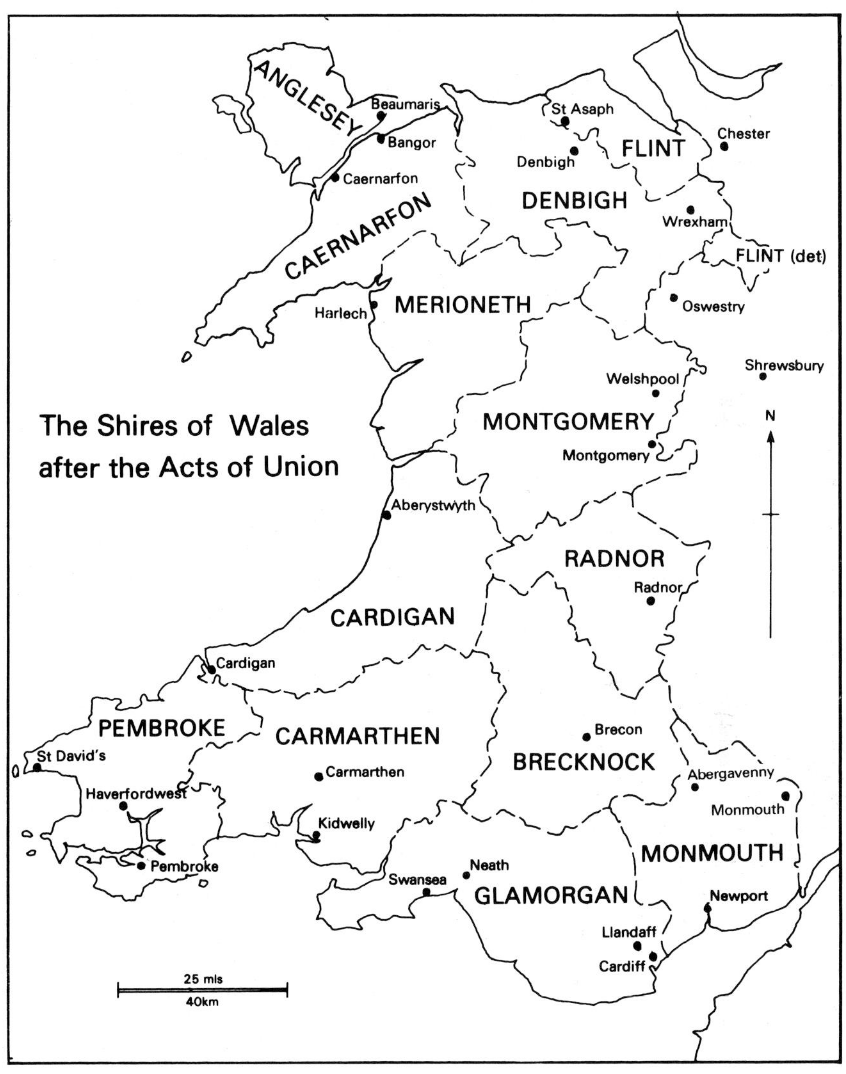
The Shires of Wales
after the Acts of Union
ANGLESEY
Beaumaris
Bangor
Caernarfon
CAERNARFON
St Asaph
Denbigh
FLINT
Chester
DENBIGH
Wrexham
FLINT (det)
Oswestry
Harlech
MERIONETH
Shrewsbury
Welshpool
N
MONTGOMERY
Montgomery
Aberystwyth
RADNOR
Radnor
CARDIGAN
Cardigan
PEMBROKE
CARMARTHEN
Brecon
St David's
BRECKNOCK
Carmarthen
Abergavenny
Haverfordwest
Monmouth
Kidwelly
MONMOUTH
Pembroke
Neath
Swansea
GLAMORGAN
Newport
Llandaff
Cardiff
25 mls
40km

achieved could the administrative changes of the 1530s be accomplished.

Just as contrary assessments have been made of the 'union' itself so have differing verdicts been passed upon the system of government that it established. Edmund Burke presented Tudor policy as a golden example of liberal rule: 'from that moment, as by a charm, the tumults subsided; obedience was restored; peace, order and civilization followed in the train of liberty.' In the twentieth century Welsh historians have condemned it as handing over the people and their culture to rapacious gentry now in control of local government: in the words of Sir Ifan ab Owen Edwards 'this uncontrolled sphere of local government became the happy hunting-ground of Welsh gentry and upstarts', who were enabled 'to intimidate, oppress and trick a monoglot people . . .'. Both views ignore the complexity of the system and of its impact.

Although Parliament remained the supreme law-making authority for Wales, it did little more after 1543 than tidy up details of the 'union' and adjudicate in local disputes. The *Privy Council* was the principal supervisory agent of government, interfering in local affairs with a constant stream of orders about matters ranging from the treatment of vagabonds to individual
E.10 thefts (E.10). Closely connected with the *Privy Council* was the *Court of Star Chamber*. This was not, in the sixteenth century, the political tribunal that it became under the Stuarts, but was a popular court for hearing cases of riot and, by extension of that jurisdiction, civil disputes. It was described by a Glamorgan gentleman who valued its protection as the 'great blazing star commonly seen at high noon within the meridian of Middlesex'. Between these central authorities and the counties were placed the two organs of regional government: the *Council in the Marches* and the *Courts of Great Sessions*. The Council acted in many ways like a combination of *Privy Council* and *Star Chamber*, being both executive agency and law-court. From its seat at Ludlow it kept a close supervisory watch upon the affairs of
E.11 Wales and the border (E.11). The *Great Sessions* were assize courts operating in four circuits, holding sessions in each Welsh county twice a year. Most of the members of the Council and most of the Sessions judges were Englishmen, living outside

Wales and able to bring relatively impartial minds to Welsh disputes.

Within the Welsh counties the system of government was patterned upon England. The principal agencies had been established by the statutes of Henry VIII, and of these the most important were the Justices of the Peace. The core of their work was done in *Quarter Sessions*, where they tried minor criminal cases and administered county affairs. Under Elizabeth they were given the task of administering the poor laws, which became one of the most important aspects of local government. In the second half of the sixteenth century the demands of national defence brought into being another local agency: the lieutenancy. Under the aegis of the President of the *Council in the Marches*, who acted as Lord-Lieutentant for the whole of Wales, deputy- lieutenants were appointed in each county with the role of commanding and training the local militia, organizing coastal defence and levying men for foreign service.

Contemporaries differed about the success of this system as later historians have done. Dr David Lewis, a judge in the Court of Admiralty, criticized the state of Wales in 1576, particularly condemning the disorders created by the retainers of gentlemen
E.12 (E.12). By implication he attacked the lenient policy of the President of the Marcher Council, Sir Henry Sidney. The counter to this was delivered by William Gerard, Chief Justice of Chester. Gerard was not uncritical of the deficiencies of Welsh government, but he mounted a powerful defence of Sidney's rule
E.13 (E.13). There is plenty of evidence to support Lewis's charges about disorderly retainers. The gentry of Glamorgan were much preoccupied with feuds during the reign of Elizabeth, culminating in bloody affrays in Cardiff between 1595 and 1597, when at least two men were killed. In Montgomery, Richard Herbert, father of Lord Herbert of Cherbury, was assaulted in Llanerfyl churchyard and 'his skull was cut through to the *pia mater* of the brain'. Such disputes can be found in every county in Wales. But gradually the hierarchy of law-courts, particularly *Star Chamber* and the *Council in the Marches*, was coming to control the violence. Litigation came to replace the riots of retainers. After the suppression of the Cardiff riots in 1597, Glamorgan seems to have been largely peaceable until the Civil War.

Sir Henry Sidney in 1573. (Artist unknown.) (*Source: National Portrait Gallery.*)

Just as the great Marcher lords had been excluded from government, so they ceased to dominate politics in Elizabethan Wales. There were still powerful noble landowners: families such as the Somersets, Earls of Worcester, the Herberts, Earls of Pembroke, the Devereux, Earls of Essex. But they had come to be principally seated in England; and although their Welsh lands provided them with local influence, a great deal of their power was derived from their position at the royal Court. Much of their political manoeuvring in Elizabethan Wales was thus an extension of the faction struggles of the English Court; and the rest was conducted within the local arenas of the shires. In that sense there was no 'Welsh politics' during the late Tudor period.

In the early part of Elizabeth's reign, until the death of Robert Dudley, Earl of Leicester, in 1588, politics at Court were fairly fluid and the factions very loosely defined. Within Wales there were several powerful figures building up local and regional influence, but no evidence of major faction-fights covering more than one county. The dominant figure was the royal favourite, Leicester, who had been granted lands in Denbighshire and Snowdonia, and built up a substantial following in north Wales. Through his brother-in-law, Sir Henry Sidney, Lord President of the *Council in the Marches* from 1560 until 1586, and Sidney's son-in-law, the Earl of Pembroke, Leicester was well placed to develop a powerful network of patronage. Only two important men remained firmly outside his orbit: Sir Richard Bulkeley of Beaumaris, who opposed Leicester's ambitions in Snowdonia; and Sir James Croft, a major Herefordshire landowner and Comptroller of the Royal Household. Neither was able to do much to shake Leicester's pervasive influence.

After 1588 rivalry at Court between the Cecils, father and son, and Robert Devereux, Earl of Essex, Leicester's stepson and the new favourite of Elizabeth, became intense. The lines between the factions became much more sharply drawn and the resulting conflicts more intense. The feuds rapidly spilled over into Wales, where Essex's interest clashed with that of Henry Herbert, Earl of Pembroke, the new Lord President of the *Council in the Marches*. Essex had inherited lands in south-west Wales and in Radnorshire, and began to build a following in Denbighshire. His supporters came from those families excluded from royal

Robert Dudley, Earl of Leicester, *c.*1575. (Artist unknown). (*Source: National Portrait Gallery.*)

favour by the Cecils and from the soldiers who served under him at Cadiz and in Ireland. Essex's principal concern was to build up a large body of influential clients and to secure for them offices in county government. In 1591 the Queen ordered that no retainer to any nobleman could hold the post of JP. Essex's indignant
E.14 response illuminates the nature of his interest (E.14). By 1601 eight of his close followers had achieved the post of deputy-lieutenant in Wales and the border. The Earl of Pembroke sulked at Essex's success. But early in 1601 Essex and his friends attempted a palace revolution in London and were humiliatingly defeated. With the execution of the Earl his faction collapsed.

The feuds at county level usually sprang from local rivalries, although they were often linked to the conflicts of courtiers. In the autumn of 1601, about six months after the death of Essex, writs for the parliamentary election were sent out, leading to a bitter conflict in Denbighshire. The county was divided between its western and eastern halves, with Sir John Salusbury of Lleweni predominant in the west and the followers of Essex — Sir Richard Trevor of Trevalun, Sir John Lloyd of Bodidras, and a *cadet* branch of the Salusburys, seated at Rug — controlling the east. There had been trouble at a previous election in 1588, and increasingly bitter conflict thereafter as Trevor and Lloyd shone in the warm glow of Essex's patronage. After a good deal of preliminary canvassing and the shift of venue from the town of Denbigh in the west to Wrexham in the east, Trevor used his powers as deputy-lieutenant to levy forty of Salusbury's supporters for military service in Ireland, thus depriving them of a voice in the election. Salusbury riposted by threatening to send to the wars any man who refused to vote for him. On election day Trevor and his friends assembled some six hundred armed men — almost certainly an exaggerated estimate — and entered Wrexham at their head, to be met by Salusbury in similar style. Next day armed conflict was only just avoided and the sheriff prudently postponed the election. Eight weeks later, just before Parliament was dissolved, Sir John Salusbury was elected; but the feud continued. Its origin essentially lay in county feuds, but these were sharpened by the intrusion of Essex on to the scene and by the set-piece contest of a parliamentary election.

In south Wales the problem of repairing Cardiff bridge reflects a different kind of dispute. The costs were high and the town insisted that the whole county was responsible. The county leaders, Sir Edward Mansell and Sir Thomas Carne, denied any legal responsibility but offered an *ex gratia* payment. In 1581 Cardiff corporation brought a bill to parliament which saddled the shire with the full costs. They secured the support, not only of William Mathew, MP for Glamorgan, but also the Earl of Pembroke, the lord of Cardiff. The gentry of the shire were determined not to be saddled with legal responsibility, since this might make them liable for the repair of all other bridges in Glamorgan. Deserted by their own MP, they turned to the major courtiers for help, appealing to the *Privy Council*, the Earl of Leicester, the Earl of Pembroke and Sir Henry Sidney. Pembroke was already committed against them and he ensured that neither Sidney, his father-in-law, nor Leicester, his uncle, would intervene. When Mansell accused Pembroke of bad faith he received a stinging rebuke from Leicester. The affair shows the rivalry among the gentry, with William Mathew, Knight of the Shire, taking sides with the town against his enemy Mansell; it also illustrates the links between local feuds and the royal Court, with the leaders of the shire turning to courtiers for help in swaying Parliament.

By the late sixteenth and early seventeenth centuries many of the Welsh gentry were commending Tudor rule in Wales, comparing the unhappy state of the county before the 'union' with its present settled condition. Sir John Wynn in Caernarfonshire, Lord Herbert of Cherbury in Montgomery, *George Owen* in Pembrokeshire and *Rice Merrick* in Glamorgan all
E.15 pointed to this happy contrast (E.15). Members of the gentry class, they were certainly beneficiaries of Tudor rule and their words are accordingly biased. Even so, Tudor rule had at least established a working system of law-courts in place of the Marcher jurisdictions, where the judicial sessions were usually a device for exacting money. The supervision of affairs by the *Privy Council*, *Star Chamber* and the *Council in the Marches*, prevented the county gentry from ruling with a completely free hand; and the worst perversions of justice do seem to have been checked.

## Sources

E.1 a) All Wales is in great decay, especially as to the breed of cattle, and the evil cannot be amended until these four articles are enforced; 1) that the officers in Wales be restrained from taking fines for felony and murder;* 2) that they may be compelled to restore tracks;** 3) that the retinue of the officers in commission with the Princess's Council do not, as now, delay justice; 4) that yearling calves be not sold.

I desire that such a Council be established in *the Marches* that the best officer in Wales shall quake if found in default.

(Thomas Phillips to Thomas Cromwell. Ludlow. 3 May 1532. *Letters and Papers of Henry VIII*, Vol.V No.991)

* i.e. that felony and murder be punished by death and not fines.

** tracks – the custom of following the tracks of stolen cattle.

b) Wales is far out of order and there have been many murders in Oswestry and Powys. No punishment has followed, because the chief of the Council are spiritual men, and cannot administer punishment of death for felony and murder. [I wish that] some man be sent down to use the sword of justice where he shall see cause throughout the principality; otherwise the Welsh will wax so wild it will not be easy to bring them into order again.

(Sir E. Croft to T. Cromwell. Ludlow. 7 March 1533; *Letters and Papers*, VI No.210)

c) More than 100 have been slain in *the Marches* of Wales since the Bishop of Exeter was President there,* and not one of them punished . . . My neighbour th'Abbot of Wigmore were bound to pray for you, if ye would write unto him to reform himself and his brothers; for in my conscience there is no worse rule kept within England nor Wales than is there kept there of all hands.

(Thomas Croft to T. Cromwell. London. 6 August 1533; *Letters and Papers*, VI No.946)

* Bishop Veysey or Voysey of Exeter became President of the *Council in the Marches* in 1526.

E.2 These shalbe t'advertise you that we have received from you the two outlaws . . . for the which we heartily thank you. And the said two outlaws we have sent to their trial according to justice, which tomorrow they shall receive (God pardon their souls). And further, within two days after the receiving of the said thieves, were brought to us four other outlaws . . . and two of the first of them had been outlawed these sixteen years. Whereof three were alive, and one slain brought in a sack trussed upon a horse, whom we have caused to be hanged upon the gallows here for a sign. Would God ye had seen the fashion thereof: it chanced the same day to be market day here, by reason whereof, 300 people followed to see the said carriage of the said thief in the sack, the manner whereof had not been seen heretofore . . . All the thieves in Wales quake with fear . . there is but one thief of name of the sort of outlaws, . . . trusting to have him shortly . . . So that now we may boldly affirm that Wales is redact to that state that one thief taketh another . . .

(Bishop Rowland Lee to T. Cromwell. 19 January 1536. *Y Cymmrodor* xiii. 125–6.)

E.3 Forasmuch as the people of Wales and *Marches* of the same, not dreading the good and wholesome laws and statutes of this realm, have of long time continued and persevered in perpetration and commission of divers and manifold thefts, murthers, rebellions, wilful burnings of houses and other scelerous deeds and abominable malefacts, to the high displeasure of God, inquietation of the King's well-disposed subjects, and disturbance of the publick weal, which malefacts and scelerous deeds be so rooted and fixed in the same people, that they be not like to cease, unless some sharp correction and punishment for redress and amputation of the premisses be provided, according to the demerits of the offenders.

(The bill concerning councils in Wales. 26 Henry VIII, c.6. 1534; Ivor Bowen, *The Statutes of Wales*, p.54.)

E.4 Where divers of the most ancient prerogatives and authorities of justice appertaining to the imperial crown of this realm have been severed and taken from the same by sundry gifts of the King's most noble progenitors, kings of this realm, to the great diminution and detriment of the royal estate of the same and to the hindrance and great delay of justice; for reformation whereof be it enacted by the authority of this present Parliament that no person or persons . . . shall have any power or authority to pardon or remit any treasons, murders, manslaughters or any kinds of felonies . . . or any outlawries for any such offences afore rehearsed, committed, perpetrated, done or divulged, or hereafter to be committed, done or divulged by or against any person or persons in any parts of this realm, Wales, or the marches of the same; but that the King's highness, his heirs and successors kings of this realm, shall have the whole and sole power and authority thereof united and knit to the imperial crown of this realm, as of good right and equity it apertaineth, any grants, usages, prescription, act or acts of Parliament, or any other thing to the contrary thereof notwithstanding.

(An act for recontinuing of certain liberties and franchises heretofore taken from the crown. 27 Henry VIII, c.24. 1536; G.R. Elton, *The Tudor Constitution*, p.37.)

E.5 Albeit the dominion principality and country of Wales justly and righteously is, and ever hath been incorporated annexed united and subject to and under the imperial crown of this realm, as a very member and joint of the same, whereof the King's most Royal Majesty . . . is very head king lord and ruler; yet notwithstanding, because that in the same country principality and dominion divers rights usages laws and customs be far discrepant from the laws and customs of this realm, and also because that the people of the same dominion have and do daily use a speech nothing like, nor consonant to the natural mother tongue used within this realm, some rude and ignorant people have made distinction and diversity between the King's subjects of this realm and his subjects of the said dominion and principality of Wales, whereby great discord variance debate division murmur and sedition hath grown between his said subjects; His Highness therefore, of a singular zeal love and favour that he beareth towards his subjects of his said dominion of Wales, minding and intending to reduce them to the perfect order notice and knowledge of his laws of this his realm, and utterly to extirp all and singular the sinister usages and customs differing from the same, and to bring the said subjects of this his realm, and of his said dominion of Wales, to an amicable concord and unity, hath by the deliberate advice consent and agreement of the Lords spiritual and temporal, and the Commons in this present Parliament assembled, and by the authority of the same, ordained enacted and established, that his said country or dominion of Wales shall be, stand and continue for ever from henceforth incorporated united and annexed to and with this his realm of England; and that all and singular person and persons, born or to be born in the said principality country or dominion of Wales, shall have enjoy and inherit all and singular freedoms liberties rights privileges and laws within this his realm, and other the King's dominions, as other the King's subjects naturally born within the same have, enjoy and inherit.

(An act for laws and justice to be ministered in Wales in like form as it is in this realm. 27 Henry VIII, c.26. 1536; Bowen, *Statutes*, pp.75–6.)

E.6 Also be it enacted by the authority aforesaid, that all justices commissioners sheriffs coroners *escheators* stewards and their lieutenants, and all other officers and ministers of the law, shall proclaim and keep the sessions courts hundreds leets, sheriffs courts, and all other courts in the English tongue; and all oaths of officers juries and inquests, and all other affidavits verdicts and wagers of law, to be given and one in the English tongue; and also that from henceforth no person or persons that use the Welsh speech or language shall have or enjoy any manner office or fees within this realm of England, Wales, or other the King's dominion, upon pain of forfeiting the same offices or fees, unless he or they use and exercise the English speech or language.

(27 Henry VIII, c.26; Bowen, *Statutes*, p.87.)

E.7 I was lately informed that the King wished to make Wales shire ground, and to have justices of the peace and gaol delivery as in England. I cannot do less than declare my mind in one point, especially as in trial of felons; for if they may come to their trials at home, where one thief shall try another, as before the last statute in that party provided they did, then that as we here have begun is foredone. You cannot do the Welshmen more pleasure than to break that statute. I would I had an hour to speak my mind to you. I think it not expedient to have justices of the peace and gaol delivery in Wales, for there are very few Welsh in Wales above Brecknock who have 10 pounds land, and their discretion is less than their land. As there is yet some bearing of the thieves by gentlemen, if this statute go forward, you will have no other but bearing and little justice . . .

(Rowland Lee to T. Cromwell. Ludlow. 12 March 1536; *Letters and Papers*, X No.453.)

E.8 Item, that there shall be and remain a President and Council in the said dominion and principality of Wales, and *the Marches* of the same, with all officers, clerks and incidents to the same, in manner and form as hath been heretofore used and accustomed; which president and council shall have power and authority to hear and determine, by their wisdoms and discretions, such causes and matters as be or hereafter shall be assigned to them by the King's Majesty, as heretofore hath been accustomed and used.

(34 & 35 Henry VIII, c.26; Bowen, *Statutes*, p.102.)

E.9 Provided always, that all lands tenements and hereditaments, within the said dominion of Wales, shall descend to the heirs, according to the course of the common laws of the realm of England, according to the tenor and effect of this act, and not to be used as *gavelkind*; any thing contained in these provisions or any of them to the contrary thereof notwithstanding.

(34 & 35 Henry VIII, c.26; Bowen, *Statutes*, p.132.)

E.10 In consequence of the benefit from the diligent execution last year of the laws against vagabonds and sturdy beggars and the disorders of the last winter resultant on less strict carrying out of these laws, you, with the justices of the peace, are again ordered to be more diligent within the next three months of August, September and October. On the 20th August, strict watch is to be kept, as well as throughout the shires as in places exempt, from 7 p.m. to 3 o'clock next afternoon by constables and two, three or more of the most substantial parishioners. All rogues, vagabonds and masterless men are to be arrested and punished by stocking and sharp and severe whipping according to the laws, afterwards sending them on, from constable to constable, until they reach their native place or last abode within three years according to the statute.

(Privy Council to Justices of the Peace. 30 July 1571; R. Flenley, *A Calendar of the Register of the Council in the Marches of Wales*, p.9.)

E.11 The Vice-president and Council now making their abode at Ludlow castle for the administration of justice, understand that tomorrow, a great fair is to be kept within the town, whereto many of her Majesty's subjects will resort for good intent to use traffic and to buy and sell. Even so in respect to the fair and to this Council many evil disposed persons will come to pick and steal and to use some shifts and disordered trade, or to flight and quarrel rather than for any good intent, for preventing whereof the Vice-president and Council have called the bailiffs of the town before them and warned them to look well to their charge. And although the Council think that they will not be forgetful of their duties for due execution of the laws against offenders, yet for more security thereof it is ordered that a letter rehearsing the premises be sent to them. Letting them know that the Council think they shall do good service to her Majesty this night in secret order upon conference amongst their brethren the aldermen and Council to enter into suspect houses for the apprehension of offenders, causing a substantial watch to be kept. Such as shall be found offenders against the laws they shall punish or else send them to the Council with certificate of their offence. And whereas many persons disposed to fighting and brawling will come to the fair bearing upon them 'gleves', spears, javelins and pikestaves so long as to be monstrous to behold, it is very meet that the bailiffs should make proclamation that no man shall bear any armour or weapons in affray of the people; and if they find any such weapon above 6 feet long they shall use their discretion to reduce it to a reasonable length.

(Order by the *Council in the Marches* at Ludlow, 24th November, 1576, in Flenley, *Register*, p.157.)

E.12 My country is so far out of order at this time as doth require severe remedy, and in every commonwealth severity used with indifferency of justice to all men is more commended than lenity . . . In my country this medicine hath been tried in Bishop Rowland [Lee's] and Mr Englefields's time, . . . and seeing experience is counted the best mistress, in my opinion, she is to be followed . . . If I might have some good laws or orders made for a better government in my country and they lived to observe them with effect, I could be content to banish myself from thence during my life . . . One thing more is to be remembered and that is the late inordinate and unlawful assembly in Glamorganshire and the excessive number of retainers there, and lest the same breed a worse example if some punishment do not ensue.

(David Lewis to Francis Walsingham, 3rd January, 1576. *Y Cymmrodor*, xiii. pp.129–30.)

Information of the disorders of Wales, 1576.
The great disorders in Wales specially in South Wales have grown much of late days, by retainers of gentlemen, whom they must after the manner of the country bear out in all actions be they never so bad.

They have also foster brothers loitering and idle kinsmen, and other hangers on, that do nothing else but play at cards and dice, and pick and steal and kill or hurt any man when they will have them and yet they themselves will wash their hands thereof when the ill fact is done.

These idle loiterers when they have offended will be shifted off to some friends of theirs in another quarter, so as they will not be found to be punished when time shall require . . .

The authority of the Council there is not regarded as it hath been . . .

(Dr David Lewis's discourse: Information of the disorders of Wales, 1576. *Y Cymmrodor*, xiii. 130–1.)

E.13 At this day it is to be affirmed that in Wales universally are as civil people and obedient to law as are in England. Throughout Wales in every respect justice embraced and with as indifferent trials executed in as England, during the time of Her Majesty's reign except 3 or 4 petty coiners; no treason heard of; very seldom murder. In 6 years together unneth [scarcely] one robbery (committed by the high way) heard of; stealing of cattle is the chief evil that generally most annoyeth the country.

(William Gerard to F. Walsingham. 20 January 1576. *Y Cymmrodor*, xiii. pp.148–9.)

E.14 Although I am very loth to leave the name of master to so many honest gentlemen in Wales, as out of their love desire to serve and follow me, and as hold the place of justices in those parts; yet I had rather give them liberty and free them from *retaining* unto me than that in this respect they should lose any jot of their former reputations; which I do with due regard to Her Majesty's service, and the good of the several counties where they dwell, being all of them, to my knowledge, very able and sufficient gentlemen. It shall therefore suffice henceforth that I have their love without further ceremonies, praying your lordship that they may not by the late order be subject to the loss of their places for this cause.

(Earl of Essex to Lord Keeper Puckering. July, 1597; P. Williams, *Council in the Marches*, p.286.)

E.15 [The author states that he is going to review the history of Wales before and during the reign of Henry VIII, so that . . . ] I might see and perceive the miserable and lamentable estate of that poor afflicted nation and country in former time, as well in subduing of the country by fire and sword and the continual thrall thereof for many years by the misgoverned governors of each several province, country or lordship thereof, rather endeavouring themselves to live upon the spoil and fleece of the poor people than to see them well governed and their oppressions redressed. Therein also appeareth the happy reforming of the said government in the time of Henry the Eighth by reducing the same into shires and in providing sweet and wholesome laws for the government thereof that comparing the present government of Wales with the government of the rest of this realm I find ourselves now in far better estate than any other part thereof governed with more ease and less charge . . .

(George Owen, *Dialogue of the Government of Wales*, H. Owen, ed., *The History of Pembrokeshire*, 1892, p.3.)

This alteration of government is worthy of remembrance as well for the singular commodity the inhabitants of Wales receive thereby as the commonwealth universally; for how unorderly they were then governed — life and death, lands and goods, subject to the pleasure of peculiar lords; and how uncertain laws, customs and usages, whereof some rested in memory and not written, were ministered a great number that live at this day can well remember and testify.

In what brickle and unstable estate men stood in those days! For the roads, incursions and slaughters between countries are not forgotten of such as now live; and, in the elder time, the treaties of the princes of Wales are a sufficient witness. Hereof it came to pass that the kings of England, at sundry times, with great armies, invaded Wales to the great disquietness of the Realm of England, and small gain to Wales, as the chronicles of England and the said treaties testify.

Now, since Wales was thus, by gracious King Henry VIII, enabled with the laws of England, and thereby united to the same, and so brought to a monarchy, which is the most sure, stable and best regiment, they are exempted from the dangers before remembered; for now life and death, lands and goods rest in this monarchy, and not in the pleasure of the subject.

Laws whereby they are governed are written, and therefore more certain to be truly and indifferently ministered.

What was then justifiable by might, although not by right, is now to receive condign punishment by law.

The discord between England and Wales, then, procured slaughters, invasions, enmities, burnings, poverty and such like fruits of war. This unity engendered friendship, amity, love, alliance, [ . . . ] assistance, wealth and quietness. God preserve and increase it.

(Rice Merrick, *Morganiae Archaiographia*, 1983, ed. Brian Ll. James, pp.67–8.)

## Debating the Evidence

Arguably, this topic is the most fully documented aspect of life in Tudor Wales. A central concern of monarch and citizens was that government should proceed efficiently and peacefully, although there are many minor occasions on which it lapsed into being neither.

The result is that the range of documents is considerable — monarch's state papers, records of institutions of government such as the *Council in the Marches*, Acts of Parliament and, inevitably, assessment of administrative changes by the ubiquitous contemporary commentators, *George Owen* and *Rice Merrick*.

*Source E.1*
Are there any reasons why Thomas Phillips and Thomas Croft might be exaggerating the extent of disorder in Wales in 1532, bearing in mind that they are writing to *Thomas Cromwell*? What weaknesses in the administration of justice are highlighted by the two writers?

*Source E.2*
What does this document reveal about some Tudor bishops?

*Source E.3*
We normally consider the direct, intentional evidence of Acts of Parliament to be completely reliable. Such Acts set out what Parliament intends to happen. However, Tudor Acts of Parliament normally have preambles such as this which set out reasons for the legislation which follows. Is there any reason why we should be suspicious about the picture which this preamble to an Act of Parliament paints of Wales in 1534?

*Source E.4*
The legal jargon of acts of parliament is always difficult to contend with, but what historical terms and events alluded to here do we need to be clear about before making good use of this document?

*Source E.6*
Compare this section of an Act with Source E.3. How does it bear out the point made that Acts of Parliament provide excellent evidence for the historian? Is this Act outlawing the use of the Welsh language for everybody?

*Source E.7*
You will see if you look at Source A.3 again that Gwynfor Jones uses part of exactly the same source. How does his use of it differ from that of Penry Williams? How far does this longer extract modify the meaning of the shorter one, if at all? This is a good example of how the *questions* a historian asks of his sources are crucial to the use he makes of them.

*Source E.8*
Can you identify any apparent contradiction in this item of legislation?

*Source E.10*
The number of vagabonds and beggars increased in the Tudor period because of inflation and the growth in population. Do you think the kinds of punishment mentioned here would be effective?

*Sources E.10, E.11 and E.12*
Does the evidence in these documents necessarily amount to a condemnation of the state of law and order in Wales in the 1570s? In what ways *might* they be construed as evidence of increasingly effective law and order? You will notice that Dr David Lewis refers to Rowland Lee. On the basis of what you have learnt of Lee's attitude do you agree with Lewis's judgement in E.12?

*Source E.13*
How might it be possible to reconcile the evidence of this document with that of the previous three documents? How might a knowledge of the background and status of William Gerard help us in this?

*Source E.14*
The Earl of Essex was, in the closing years of the sixteenth century, until his execution in 1601, one of the most influential members of the aristocracy in the country. He built up an important network of gentry connections in west Wales. Why should he do this? Is this evidence of Essex's to be trusted? What does it tell us about the position of the great aristocratic figures of the political life of the period?

*Source E.15*
In what ways do these accounts of government in Elizabethan Wales agree? How would our interpretation of these accounts be influenced by the knowledge of who *George Owen* and *Rice Merrick* were — both landed

Henry Herbert, second Earl of Pembroke (*c.* 1534–1601). (Artist unknown). (*Source: National Museum of Wales.*)

gentlemen, both playing an important part in the government and administration of their counties? Why should they be so favourably disposed to the Union settlement of 1536–1543? Is there any way in which their view of events and that presented by Dr David Lewis in E.12 can be reconciled?

## Discussion

No legislation in Welsh history has been as contentious as that of 1536–1543 which united the 'Dominion, Principality and Country of Wales', to use the words of the 1536 Act, with England. In retrospect we know that the Union was to prove permanent, at least to the present. The elevation of Welshmen to the ranks of equality with English citizens (E.5) provides an impressively successful example of racial integration. The shires mooted in 1536 and consolidated in 1543 formed the unit of local government in Wales until 1974. The system of courts by which justice was administered at county level continued until the nineteenth century. The ordinary citizens of sixteenth-century Wales of course had no hand in devising the terms according to which they were to be governed. It was over 500 years before the Welsh were to be consulted on the principle of full-scale union when in 1979, they were offered a partial untying of the sixteenth- century knot. The Welsh endorsed unity.

This brings us once more to a central dilemma in the historian's craft. In my remarks I have collated Tudor union with twentieth-century unity. Is this not unhistorical? Surely so much has changed during the intervening half millenium that it is wholly inappropriate? And yet historical union with England is a constant theme of nationalist writing and the implications of union are still central to the Welsh nation and people even if the circumstances and context have been comprehensively modified. The only answer for the historian of Wales must be that the constant analysis of present-day Wales, politically and linguistically, in terms of the events of Tudor times, is a fact of life and itself will become a part of the history of that union. At the same time, the historian's training, his regard for evidence, must distinguish him from those who seek to use the past for present purposes of polemic or propaganda, laudable as we may feel the purpose to be. It is the historian's task to try to analyse the union of England and Wales, its immediate successes and failures, in Tudor terms and not in twentieth century terms. This is no easy task, as will be apparent from the corpus of evidence which Penry Williams provides. The evidence of disorders in Wales is unequivocal. Wales was a lawless country in the 1530s (E.1, E.2). Or was it? It could be that those religious changes which were discussed in the previous section were such a source of disquiet to the King's ministers that a level of disorder which was no greater than previously now assumed dangerous proportions. It may also have been that the King's new chief minister at this time, *Thomas Cromwell*, for adminstrative reasons, had different perceptions of the nation and the state under the monarch than those of previous ministers. Such, certainly, is the thrust of some historians' assessments of *Cromwell*. If either or both these analyses have some validity then it is easy to envisage a situation in which *Cromwell* sought for evidence of disorder in Wales and his correspondents duly supplied him with what he wanted to hear, just as his monastic Visitors provided him with damning assessments of the state of morality in the monasteries. It will be obvious from foregoing discussions that *Cromwell*'s correspondents would be people high in the social scale. It could be the case, and there is evidence for this, that their perception of the needs of Wales had changed out of self-interest. They had now come to the fore as a class, they wanted their status in society consolidated and their lifestyle protected. They wanted equality before the law (E.5) with their English compeers and the removal from the statute system of land inheritance. They had a motive for exaggerating lawlessness in Wales.

This last point is of particular significance in assessing the force of sources such as E.15. How is it possible to reconcile the picture of Wales painted by Dr David Lewis in E.12 with the eulogies to the Tudor dynasty which according to *Owen* and *Merrick* in E.15 brought peace and tranquillity to a land torn by strife and lawlessness? Dr David Lewis's Wales seems anything but a haven of good order, with retainers of gentry and aristocracy, especially, a continuing threat to peace. Source E.14 provides corroboration of the existence of these retainers, and we know from court records that the kinds of disturbance of the peace instanced by Lewis were regular occurrences. Furthermore we know that often gentlemen, that is those people who had been entrusted since the *Acts of Union* with the administration of justice in their capacity as sheriffs, Justices of the Peace and eventually deputy lieutentants, were the worst offenders. However, we also know that the 1570s were dangerous years in Tudor England and Wales and that the authority of the *Council in the Marches* had been particularly abused in recent years.

Here, then, could be an explanation for Lewis's worries about the state of Wales, and they might not indicate, indeed Tudor historians would argue they do not adequately reflect, the improvements which had taken place since the 1540s. Even so, the discrepancy between Lewis's evidence and the accounts of Gerard in E.13 and *Owen* and *Merrick* in E.15 is startling. If Lewis's perception of the scale of disorder might be exaggerated, why should other accounts of the scale of good order be distorted? The answer here is, as always, the bias of the observer, and points to the necessity for investigating the background to the author of any piece of historical documentation but especially literary pieces such as these. *George Owen* and *Rice Merrick* were gentlemen. As such they were members of that group which had benefitted most from Henry VIII's Union legislation. It had set the seal on the economic changes of the previous century which had brought these families to prominence and it had given respectability to their position by bringing them into partnership in the government and administration of their communities. Not surprisingly, they looked favourably on the *Acts of Union*. Not surprisingly, they regarded the system of local government of which they were the mainstays as responsible for a dramatic improvement, even a transformation, in law and order in Wales. That is the picture which they draw in their evidence. Given the authorship of the sources such a picture should occasion no surprise. Their evidence provides a stark reminder of the bias present in all historical sources to a greater or lesser extent and the necessity for historians to exercise great care as they evaluate such sources.

# *Further Reading*

If you have no knowledge at all of the history of the sixteenth century in Wales it would be most useful to familiarize yourself with the main events. You might read Hugh Thomas, *A History of Wales 1485–1660* (Cardiff, University of Wales Press, 1972) or the first part of Gareth Elwyn Jones, *Modern Wales* (Cambridge, Cambridge University Press, 1984) or the relevant essays in *Wales through the Ages* edited by A.J. Roderick (Llandybie, Christopher Davies, 1960). General economic history is covered in Joan Thirsk (ed.) *The Agrarian History of England and Wales*, Vol.IV, 1500–1640 (Cambridge, Cambridge University Press, 1967), while Brian Howells has published numerous other essays on topics he deals with here, including 'Pembrokeshire Farming' in the *National Library of Wales Journal* for 1956. G.D. Owen's, *Elizabethan Wales: The Social Scene* (Cardiff, University of Wales Press, 1962) has chapters on town and country life.

The essential book on religious changes in Tudor Wales is Glanmor Williams, *Welsh Reformation Essays* (Cardiff, University of Wales Press, 1967). The major work on Tudor administration is Penry Williams, *The Council in the Marches of Wales under Elizabeth I*, (Cardiff, University of Wales Press, 1958). Gareth Jones's *The Gentry and the Elizabethan State* (Pbk. edition, Llandybie, Christopher Davies, 1984) deals with the gentry's role in administration.

# *Glossary*

| | |
|---|---|
| *Acts of Union* | A series of Acts, the most important of which were passed in 1536 and 1543, which united Wales with England. |
| *Arthur* | Henry VII's eldest son and heir, who died before becoming King. |
| *Bardic order* | See *Bards*. |
| *Bards* | Poets who were in practice custodians of Welsh history and tradition and occupied honoured positions in princely and gentry households. |
| *Bastides* | Small fortified towns on a grid pattern built by the Normans. |
| *Battle of Bosworth* | Fought between Richard III and Henry Tudor in 1485, as a result of which Henry Tudor became King as Henry VII. |
| *Bond hamlets* | Part of the organization of medieval Welsh social and economic life. The lower orders in Welsh society consisted of bondsmen whose position in society was roughly equivalent to that of the *villein*. Their freedom was restricted and they provided labour services. |
| *Bond tenancy* | See *Bond hamlets*. |
| *Bosworth Field* | See *Battle of Bosworth*. |
| *Burgage plots* | Areas of land in a borough — a town which had received a charter. |

| | |
|---|---|
| *Burgess* | Leading citizens in the boroughs. A borough was a town which had a charter. |
| *Cadet houses* | Gentry families established by younger sons. |
| *Cadets* | Younger sons of gentry families. |
| *Cadwaladr* | Regarded as the last King of the Britons. |
| *Camden, William* (1551–1623) | An outstanding antiquary whose *Britannia* is an excellent description of the places he visited and is an invaluable source for the early modern historian. |
| *Caput* | Head or top — chief castle of a lordship. |
| *Chancery for Wales* | An important court which developed in England in the fifteenth century. It could make law. It dealt with land ownership and contract cases. |
| *Chantries* | Small chapels, set up from medieval times by individual endowments, mainly for the purpose of saying masses for the dead. |
| *Clanland* | Community land. |
| *Clanlands* | Lands belonging to groups of related individuals in the kindred system. |
| *Commote* | In Welsh law a commote was an area which contained fifty small townships or villages. |
| *Copyhold* | A form of manorial tenure. |
| *Council in the Marches* | Administrative and judicial body created in 1471 but given statutory existence by the *Acts of Union*. |
| *Courts of Great Sessions* | Courts of law established by the *Acts of Union* and gave twelve of the Welsh counties a distinctive system of justice. |
| *Court of Star Chamber* | The most important court in England and Wales. Roughly, the *Privy Council* sitting as a court. |

| | |
|---|---|
| *Cromwell, Thomas* (*c*.1485–1540) | Henry VIII's second great chief minister. The first was Thomas Wolsey. |
| *Crown bond townships* | See *Bond tenancy*. |
| *Custom of the manor* | Leases by which land was held. Originally these were agreed between lord and tenant, but in time became customary. |
| *Custumals* | Lists of *customs of the manor*. |
| *Cyfran* | Division of land between male heirs. |
| *Cymorth/Cymortha* | The practice of mutual help in the community . Originated in need for co-operative labour in the countryside. Had been corrupted to financial exactions by Marcher lords. |
| *Demesnes* | That area of land which was worked directly by the lord of the manor's servants. |
| *Dissolution of the monasteries* | Henry VIII closed down the Roman Catholic monasteries in the 1530s. This was partly a consequence of his break with Rome, but mainly because he coveted their great wealth. |
| *Empty bond vills* | Areas of settlement which had gone out of cultivation due to depopulation among bondsmen. |
| *Encroachment* | The process by which land was taken over bit by bit by neighbouring landowners. |
| *Englishries* | Areas in Wales which had been settled by the English, as opposed to 'Welshries'. |
| *Escheat* | Lands which reverted to the lord of the manor by, for example, right of wardship (administration of the land of minors). |
| *Feudal dues* | Dues owed to a lord of the manor by his tenants. |
| *Ffridd/Ffriddoedd* | Mountain pastures or sheep walks. |
| *Fiefs* | Land held in return for homage and services (normally military). |

| | |
|---|---|
| *Friezes* | Coarse woollen cloth. |
| *Gascony* | A region of south-west France. |
| *Gavelkind* | See *Cyfran*. |
| *Glyndŵr Revolt* | See *Owain Glyndŵr*. |
| *Great Sessions* | See *Courts of Great Sessions*. |
| *Hafotai* | Temporary shelters used by herdsmen when the cattle went to summer pasture. |
| *Historia Regum Britanniae* | A history of the Kings of Britain, written by Geoffrey of Monmouth in 1136. |
| *Hundredal Juries* | Each county was divided into hundreds and each hundred held its own court for minor offences. Juries played an important part in these courts. |
| *Hundreds* | See *Hundredal Juries*. |
| *Husbandmen* | Ranked on the social scale below *yeomen*. Normally rented land up to perhaps 30 acres. |
| *Infilling* | The process of building on land within town walls. |
| *Jacobean* | Pertaining to the reign of King James I. |
| *Kindred system* | A system of land holding by groups of kinsmen with a common ancestor. |
| *Kulaks* | Prosperous Russian peasants. |
| *Leasehold* | A form of manorial land tenure. |
| *Leland, John* (1506–1552) | Henry VIII's Royal Antiquary. |
| *Manorial custom* | See *Custom of the manor*. |
| *March, The* | The area of Wales conquered by individual Norman marcher lords and held by them from the eleventh to the sixteenth century. See map, p. 138. |

| | |
|---|---|
| *Merrick, Rice* (d.1587) | of Cottrell in Glamorgan — lawyer and well-known antiquary. |
| *Morcellated* | See *Morcellation*. |
| *Morcellation* | Land divided up repeatedly by *cyfran* or *gavelkind* (qv). |
| *Mortgage* | Money obtained by providing land as security. |
| *Nucleated* | Developing around a nucleus — in this case villages developing around church and manor. |
| *Offa's Dyke* | The great earthwork constructed by Offa of Mercia at the end of the eighth century. It approximates to today's boundary between England and Wales. |
| *Owain Glyndŵr* | Rebel independent Prince of Wales in the first decade of the fifteenth century. |
| *Owen, George* (*c*.1552-1613) | — of Henllys in Pembrokeshire, one of the finest of Welsh antiquaries. |
| *Partible inheritance* | Division of land between male heirs. |
| *Poor Law of 1598* | One of a series of Elizabethan poor laws which attempted to deal with the increasing problem of poverty and vagrancy in the sixteenth century. |
| *Primogeniture* | Inheritance by the eldest son. |
| *Privy Council* | The most important administrative body in the country. Composed mainly of administrators and courtiers. |
| *Probate* | The legal scrutiny of wills. Wills are an invaluable source for sixteenth-century social historians. |
| *Quarter Sessions* | Courts which tried less important cases than courts of *Great Sessions*. Held every three months. |
| *Recusants* | Roman Catholics who refused to accept the religious settlement of Elizabeth I's reign. |

| | |
|---|---|
| *Rentier* | Someone whose income is derived from rent or investments. |
| *Restoration* | The restoration of the monarchy after the commonwealth period at the accession of King Charles II in 1660. |
| *Retaining* | Employment of bands of servants by aristocracy or gentry. Retainers were often regarded as a source of disturbance and fighting. |
| *Seigneurial demesnes* | land worked directly by the lord of the manor's servants. |
| *Serfdom* | Serfs were tied to the lord's land and went with the land when it changed ownership. |
| *Sharelands* | Open field belonging to a township or hamlet in which land is held in strips. |
| *Speed, John* (*c.*1552-1629) | The great map-maker of the early seventeenth century. |
| *Statute of Artificers* | See Document B.8. |
| *Transhumance graziers* | Farmers who transferred sheep or cattle to different pastures with changes of climate. Effectively, moving cattle and sheep in the summer season. |
| *Tuckers' guild* | Organization of lace or linen makers. |
| *Uchelwyr* | The Welsh word for gentry. |
| *Valor Ecclesiasticus* | The evaluation of ecclesiastical land carried out in 1535. |
| *Villein* | See *villein holdings*. |
| *Villein holdings* | Villeins held land by feudal tenure of lords of the manor — they had to pay rent and work on the lord's land. They were attached to the manor and could not leave without permission. Their position was roughly equivalent to that of the Welsh bondmen. |

| | |
|---|---|
| *Wallia pura* | The areas of Wales not settled by Normans or English, remaining in the hands of the native Welsh. |
| *Wars of the Roses* | Civil wars of the fifteenth century in England. |
| *Yeomen* | Came in the social and economic scale below gentry but above *husbandmen*. Technically held land worth £2 per annum and above. The lowest rank allowed to read the Bible. |

# Index